Historic
JEFFERSON CITY
HOTELS

Historic JEFFERSON CITY HOTELS

Michelle Brooks

Published by The History Press
An imprint of Arcadia Publishing
Charleston, SC
www.historypress.com

First published 2026

Manufactured in the United States

ISBN 9781467157513

Library of Congress Control Number: 2025946006

The author would like to dedicate this book to her coworkers at the Missouri State Archives for their support, suggestions, and enthusiasm.

CONTENTS

FOREWORD

From the days when legislators and other visitors arrived in Jefferson City by horseback and steamboat to the days of sleek cars and airplanes, those coming to the Missouri capital have need places to rest their weary and sometimes blurry heads.

From the days of one small hotel and tents passing as lodging to the era of modern hotels and motels with all of their amenities, lodging places have played a key role in Jefferson City's development. The common and the great have been lodgers in the town. Outlaws and statesmen—and stateswomen—have slept here, and for many years hundreds of visitors were not welcome in these places of rest.

These are the stories of the vitally important lodging industry and the people who have created history by their visits to one important town in one state in the middle of a nation.

—Bob Priddy

ACKNOWLEDGEMENTS

The author is deeply grateful for the grace and compassion extended during complications that delayed the preparation of this book, from The History Press, friends, family, and coworkers.

Thank you to Henry Gensky, who was, in part, inspiration for recording the locations, names, and stories associated with the historic hotels long gone in the "Capital City."

Historic newspapers were a heavy resource for this book. What a treasure to have lifetimes of daily news captured for future generations, first by the early newspapermen and today shared online and on microfilm at local repositories.

Photos of bygone hotels are fun to look at. But that wouldn't be possible without the foresight of people like Joseph Summers, Bob Priddy, Arnold Parks, and others who collected images and postcards that were shared with the Missouri State Archives and the Cole County Historical Society.

Many individuals contributed to this project, lending their knowledge, family stories, photos, skills, and insight. Thank you to Stephen Brooks, Ruthie Caplinger, John Dougan, Lena Evers-Hillstrom, Thomas Fales, Sue Gerber, Debbie Goldammer, Wayne Johnson, Kyrstin Keim, Mary Mitchell, Kate Owens, Tiffany Patterson, Bob Priddy, Wyatt Prosch, Gary and Doris Schmutzler, Walter Schroeder, Stephen Stark, Keith Stroessner, Darrell Strope, Nancy Arnold Thompson, Ethan Tyrrell, Patrick Wilson, and Greg Wolk.

INTRODUCTION

The frontier spirit requires tenacity and imagination. Building a capital under the constant threat of its main asset being removed called for ambition and resilience.

In the nineteenth century, growth of Jefferson City hotels and those who owned and managed them played a crucial role. However, the investment often outweighed the revenue for many of the earliest entrepreneurs.

For a few months every two years, the demand for rooms was more than the small town could provide. Boarding houses, private homes, and even tents were used to host the hundreds of elected officials and their entourages.

Jefferson City's earliest and largest buildings were often the hotels. The hotel operators faced pressure to keep up with the amenities of the St. Louis hotels. Frequent redecorating and refurnishing ran many of the early hoteliers into bankruptcy.

Those who seemed to succeed in the mid-1800s were those with an alternate revenue stream, like capitalist Thomas Lawson Price, liveryman Burr McCarty, and doctor Tennessee Mathews. Of course, the first hotel, the Rising Sun, saw early success simply by being the only inn for nearly a decade.

Those who saw longevity in the early hotel business of Jefferson City generally had support systems, either of multigenerational family members or, more often, enslaved people.

Some who briefly operated local hotels quickly discovered that they preferred farm life or moved on to larger opportunities. A few operated the hotels while family were in the legislature. Widows and single women operated boarding houses of varying size, generally out of necessity.

The coming of the Missouri Pacific Railroad in 1856 brought with it a shift from the home-style frontier inn to larger hotels focusing on more than just rooms, meals, and a saloon.

During the Civil War, hotels were full, either of officers from the occupying Union forces or with refugees fleeing guerrillas in the rural areas.

Jefferson City saw a few building booms in the years following the war, with hotels being added and improved at the same rate as commercial, residential, church, and club buildings.

The City Hotel added a third story, the Madison House introduced the first music hall, the Monroe House grew from a corner saloon, and the Central Hotel received an extra story and a facelift. While these more elite hotels lightly competed with one another for the most prestigious of guests or to host the most elite events, they were unified in pushing for the city's progress.

For some hotels, pushing for progress included installing private sewers and electricity in advance of the city system. As new technology emerged—such as elevators, air conditioning, and telephones—hotels were often the first place in town to add the innovations.

Toward the end of the nineteenth century, clientele for local hotels diversified. The second Pacific House opened across from the Missouri Pacific Depot, serving visitors as well as railroaders. And the Farmers Home and Nieghorn House in the Munichburg area welcomed new German-speaking immigrants and farmers bringing their produce to town.

For those passing through or temporarily staying in Jefferson City, the local hotels were the first impression of the Capital City. For those making Jefferson City their home, the hotels were architectural landmarks and gathering places for social and civic affairs.

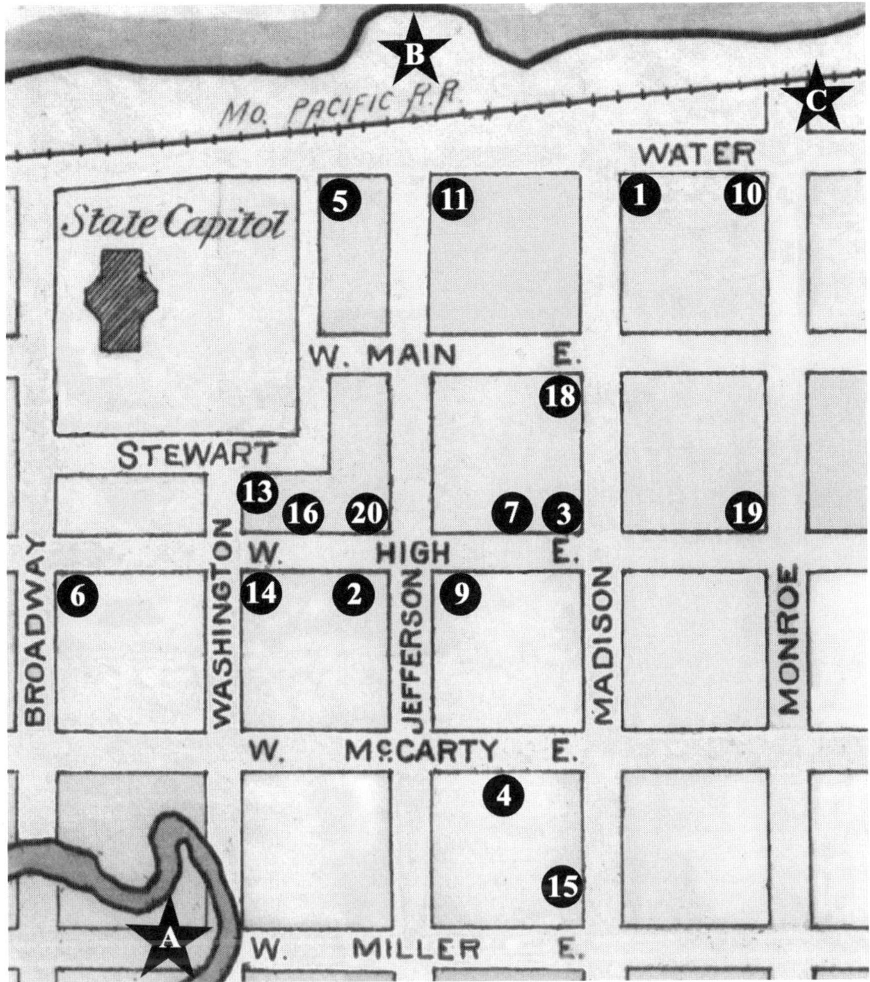

Map location of hotels mentioned in this book. *Sanborn Insurance map/Michelle Brooks.*

1. Rising Sun Hotel
2. First City Hotel, Neef House
3. Second City Hotel
4. McCarty House
5. First Missouri House
6. Ferguson House
7. Wagner Hotel
8. Virginia Hotel, Central Hotel
9. Jefferson House
10. New Pacific Hotel
11. Second Missouri Hotel
12. Tennessee House
13. Ransom-Capitol House
14. Bruns Boarding House
15. Lansdown Boarding House
16. Lusk-Nichols House
17. New City Hotel
18. Hotel Madison
19. Monroe House

A. Wiers Creek
B. City Landing
C. Missouri Pacific Depot

Part I

IN THE BEGINNING

A desolate, limestone cliff was destined to be named Missouri's capital, not because of what was there but because of its location on the Missouri River—the superhighway of the nineteenth century—near the mouth of the Osage River.

Only William Jones occupied what would become Jefferson City, with his small saloon on the riverbank near Wier's Creek. It would take five years and thirty families with their enslaved people to carve out the first streets and erect the first buildings.

Although progress had been made, converting the forested cliff into city lots, the meager village had few amenities when the Fourth General Assembly arrived with thirty-eight representatives and fourteen senators. It was November 1826, the first legislative session at Jefferson City, as the permanent seat of government.

One of those amenities was the Rising Sun Hotel, sharing the same magnificent view of the Missouri River as the recently completed statehouse. The town included six brick and two stone buildings. Next door to the first inn and across Madison Street from the statehouse was Calvin Gunn's newspaper office, and just south of that was War of 1812 veteran Israel Reed's general store. A block west on Jefferson Street was the ferry landing and gristmill. The city also had a distillery, a doctor, and a tannery. Revolutionary War veteran Christopher Casey was constable, and Josiah Ramsey, from Callaway County, was postmaster.

John Churchill Gordon Jr.'s Rising Sun Hotel offered not only beds for select few but also refreshment and a gathering place for all of these dignitaries from across the frontier state. Soon after the General Assembly's arrival, tavern licenses were issued also to Ramsey, Ralph Briscoe, and Job Goodall.

A warm meal, a little privacy, and a polite greeting were among the few comforts early visitors could find in a wilderness village growing around a new statehouse, particularly during the biennial stays of the elected state officials. Taverns and inns were the respite from, and sometimes the continuation of, the political debates and responsibilities.

One tavern keeper apparently hung a sign advertising "entertainment," but all he had was a floorless board structure with an office in front and a dining room and kitchen in the rear. When a legislator sought a room after his meal, he was taken out the backdoor by candlelight to small wooden buildings and several tents with cots inside.

Others stayed in the few modest homes of the residents. But nearly all of the early political visitors slept in tight quarters, up to three in a bed.

THE RISING SUN HOTEL

1826–1906

More than one hundred visitors arriving for a few months every two years was difficult to build a business around. Traveling salesmen and westward pioneers filled only a few beds and pints before the stagecoach (1836) and railroad (1856) arrived.

John Churchill Gordon Jr. was the first to take a risk, just as he was among the first to settle in Jefferson City after the May 1823 sale of lots. He helped shape the beginnings of Jefferson City, from overseeing the first sale of lots to seeing a road built from Marion, then the seat of Cole County, to the Capital City.

In July 1825, Gordon bought three lots facing Water Street at the corner of Madison Street for $146 (about $4,600 in 2025 dollars). Anticipating the first General Assembly in Jefferson City, Gordon and Howard County State Representative Alfred Basye made an agreement whereby Gordon would build for Basye a twenty-four-by-thirty-foot log house set on stone pillars in the 400 block of East Capitol Avenue. In exchange, Basye would give

Gordon three lots of prime real estate at the intersection of Madison at High Streets and twenty thousand bricks by September 1826. Gordon used the bricks to build his hotel, a property that Basye would own later.

As two of the greatest landowners at the time, Gordon and Basye had eyes on the future of this yet-to-be-built city when it was just hills of ancient forest.

Gordon was the oldest son of Revolutionary War veteran John Churchill Gordon Sr., who moved from Virginia to Kentucky before settling at Cote sans Dessein in Callaway County with his in-laws, including Revolutionary War Patriot Christopher Casey.

The Gordon family home was at the northwest corner of Capitol and Jackson Streets, where Buescher Funeral Home is today. Here they hosted the first Cole County Circuit Court meeting in Jefferson City after the seat was moved from Marion in 1829. Space was rented temporarily in the Gordon's home for the County Clerk's Office, and the town's board of trustees held its monthly meetings there.

The Rising Sun Hotel

Overlooking the Missouri River, Gordon built a "rambling frame structure" that got its name from its view east. The "view up and down the river was magnificent," said Frank Miller, a Basye descendent who grew up in the home. At the entrance hung a sign with "a gorgeous delineation of a rising sun in gold and curly-cues, which gave the hostelry its name," the *Kansas City Times* reported in 1891.

In an early story from the Rising Sun Hotel, the notorious John Smith T. once pulled a pistol on Major James Rollins, who refused a drink. Smith T. threatened him, saying, "My friend Gordon keeps mighty fine liquor." Rollins, despite being known for his temperance, chose the drink. Smith T. was a judge in Ste. Genevieve County well before statehood. His notoriety, however, comes from his dueling prowess, as he killed more than ten men, including Aaron Burr's nephew. All men of reputation, like Smith T., would have stopped at the Rising Sun in the city's first decades.

Looking for new entrepreneurial outlets, Gordon lost a bid in 1836 for the commissioner of the seat of government to Basye's son-in-law and future Circuit Court judge George W. Miller. But in 1838, Gordon and William S. Burch were appointed as the first private keepers of the Missouri State Penitentiary for a term of four years, replacing the state-funded warden system. That meant Gordon and Burch had to find ways to cover the costs of operations. They frequently hired out inmate labor for construction and other projects across town. Inmates made bricks from clay on site and also quarried and cut building stone, both used in construction at the prison and in many of the town's early homes.

Gordon left for the 1849 gold rush and died in California.

Alfred Basye

The Rising Sun Hotel changed hands from Gordon to Alfred Basye in 1838. Basye's father-in-law bought the property, "where travelers can at all times be accommodated," and Basye bought it in November 1839. Basye was not new to keeping an inn, having done so already in Columbia.

The sizeable Basye family of ten daughters and two sons moved into a new brick addition to the hotel in 1846. Under the care of Alfred Basye's cousin-wife, Frances de Wilton Robinson, the boarding house continued to cater to state officers and legislators. Through the Civil War, their daughters Susan and Elizabeth continued lodging working-class men. The Basye family provided boarding to Missouri's politicians for nearly fifty years.

Despite the owner's prohibition of alcohol and card-playing, the Basyes' hotel likely served as a meeting place for some of their children to find their prominent spouses. Alfred Jr. was a doctor and married Mary Walker, daughter of state treasurer John Walker. Nancy married Cyrus Stark, who published the first newspaper in Springfield. Eliza married Ben Holliday, who published the first newspaper in Howard County. Louisa married George W. Miller, longtime Cole County Circuit Court judge. Mary married Dr. Moody Mansur, a graduate of Harvard University who served in the Seminole War as army surgeon. Frances married Ambrose D. Reynolds, the only son of Governor Thomas Reynolds. Narcissa married Andrew King, St. Charles County representative and later congressman. And Margaret married Captain Sinclair Miller, a Buchanan County representative.

The Basyes came from a Virginia family of distinguished cousins, including Chief Justice John Marshall, President William Henry Harrison, and President Zachary Taylor, according to descendant Ann Stuart Dewey.

A large man at six feet tall, Basye had a pleasant face, according to the remembrances of Dr. Robert Young in *Pioneers of High, Water and Main*. Growing up playing games on Madison Street in front of the hotel, Young said that he remembered Basye to be kind, gentle, well-mannered, and popular with his neighbors.

The Basye family came before 1820 to Howard County, where Alfred was a major in the Missouri Militia and one of five state representatives in 1822 and 1824. He was president of the Presbyterian Society in Fayette when it organized in October 1824.

In November 1825, he paid $510 (about $16,200 in 2025 dollars) for sixteen city lots in Jefferson City, including the 400 block of East Main Street, where he is said to have built the city's first brick home. The Basye family brought sixty cattle, twenty horses and thirty enslaved people. Legend says that the people he enslaved made the bricks in Boone County and then hauled them by oxen and across the river to the new Capital City.

As part of the trade for John C. Gordon Jr. to build the Rising Sun Hotel, Gordon, a carpenter, built a log house, styled after a home already in the Capital City occupied by Charles Norwood. This first Basye home was twenty-four by thirty feet and nine feet high and divided into three rooms, with an attic. It reflected new improvements to the early colonial log structure, including four outside doors, twelve-pane glass windows, tongue-and-groove flooring, and a closet beneath the stairway. Part of this historic home at 420 Capitol Avenue still stood in 1962, boasting architectural features from the "Old South" and still retaining the slave quarters and carriage house.

One of the people enslaved by Basye was Balis, who managed the hotel's baggage wagon. Dr. Young recalled Balis as "a universal favorite because of his reliability, intelligence and good nature, not only among town people but the traveling public."

Basye held considerable property across town, including a majority of the land west of the Mill Bottom, which local leaders promoted as the site of a university. He also served as postmaster and commissioner of the permanent seat of government. As the latter, Basye was charged with taking care of the state's graveyard, installing a fence and gate around the capitol, improving the governor's house, leasing a cabin on the old statehouse lot, and conducting a new survey of the city.

Unmarried daughters Susan and Elizabeth continued to operate the boarding house after their parents' deaths. Their boarders included local professionals and, with its proximity to the Pacific Railroad depot, several railroad men. One of them was Charles Wray Stuart, whom Susan later married in July 1860. He had been a farmer in Marion until his first wife died in 1847. Then he moved to the city with his two sons to take work with the railroad.

Stuart shared the same southern heritage as the Basye family. Not surprising then that the hotel was the site for a local rally to show support for Missouri governor Claiborne Jackson's refusal to comply with the Union request for troops in 1861. A flag with red and white stripes and eight stars in an incomplete circle was raised. So many citizens, legislators, and their wives gathered for the event that the long gallery on the front of the Basye House was filled. This site for decades to follow had the nickname "Fort Jackson."

A Basye descendant told heroic stories about Susan during the Union occupation. East of the large home, an orchard rolled down the slope. Union soldiers were causing "depredations" to the property. Despite the Basye family being known as rebel sympathizers, the orchard was protected by the occupying officers after Susan made a personal appeal. Another time, with no male adult in the house, Susan defended her own property. She took the family saber from over the mantel and chased an intruder to the eastern limits, as Ann Stuart Dewey wrote for a 1945 *News Tribune*.

The Rising Sun Hotel was lost to fire in 1906 and replaced by a more modest brick home, where the last Basye daughters lived until their deaths. The site was considered in the 1940s for a modern hotel but today is occupied by Ameren Missouri.

Part II

1827 to 1840

Most early hotel operators in Jefferson City did not stay in the business long. Keeping first class–caliber rooms that were filled for only a few months every two years drove many into bankruptcy. Others found they preferred life on the farm, while a few moved elsewhere to operate rooming houses.

In the decades before the railroad, hotels were the leading buildings of the streetscape and often sat next to vacant, overgrown lots and fronted muddy streets. They were the public gathering spaces for locals, the first offices for many newly arrived professionals, and a place for transient salesmen. These include Madame Wordeman, music teacher, and Frederick Webb, a daguerreotype artist, each of whom stayed several weeks at the Missouri House in the 1840s.

Seven hotels, in addition to the Rising Sun, emerged for the long term in the era between the first General Assembly's meeting in Jefferson City and the safe arrival of the first train from St. Louis in 1856.

The first City Hotel opened at 111 West High Street about 1834. The White House opened about 1838 on Main Street and the McCarty House about 1839 between Madison and Jefferson Streets. The Missouri House at the city wharf and the National Hotel at northwest corner of High and Madison Streets opened by 1840. The Ferguson House opened in 1844 at the southeast corner of Broadway and High Street. Then a new standard of hotel was established on High Street with the Virginia Hotel in 1848 and the Jefferson House in 1853.

Emerging City

The city emerged from years of patience and hard work, cutting down hills, leveling streets, and establishing grades—mostly by hand and often with prisoner or slave labor. They faced hard winters, heavy spring thaws, and muddy streets that could stop a wagon. "But in spite of all this the city grew, people stayed and life went on day after day," the 1942 *News Tribune* reflected. Jefferson City was settling into the biennial rhythm of legislative visitors in the 1830s.

Regular mail routes by horseback were established to Jefferson City in 1834—once a week to and from Boonville and twice weekly to St. Louis and south. Congress expanded the postal routes in 1836, which helped develop easier access by ground to the Capital City. For the first time, mail would travel directly from Jefferson City to Versailles, Waynesville, Columbia, and others. This created the way for stagecoaches.

A separate Governor's Mansion had been built at the northwest corner of Madison and Main Streets, freeing up space within the original statehouse. And the Missouri State Penitentiary opened in 1836, further securing the permanence of state government in the city born for that purpose.

The new capitol, including a library and executive rooms, was completed in 1837. Similar to a decade earlier, dozens of builders came into the city to work. Many families in the Cole County area today can trace a family line back to someone who worked on this project. The construction project brought many changes to the community. For example, St. Peter Catholic Church saw an influx of so many Irish parishioners that it added an Irish sister to the school.

In the meantime, James Dunnica, builder of the original statehouse, constructed several other tasteful brick buildings in town. However, the best corner lots were "still encumbered with native crabtree and principal streets thickly shaded with hazel," the 1837 *Missouri Gazetteer* said.

By 1840, twenty-six steamboats were plying the waters between St. Louis and Glasgow, passing Jefferson City on the Missouri River, and three stagecoach lines were operating out of the Newman and City Hotels.

"Being permanently fixed as the seat of government for the state, which is rapidly improving in every quarter, and its eligible situation for trade and commerce, it may confidently be anticipated, that within a short period Jefferson City will rank among the foremost of the cities in the western states," the *Weekly Jefferson Inquirer* wrote.

First City Hotel

circa 1834–circa 1852

The second hotel built in the new Capital City was the City Hotel at 111 West High Street, across from Burr McCarty's livery stable. On a rise above its surroundings, the large brick building was open by 1834 and became the meeting point of the eastern and western stages.

The hotel temporarily held the federal District Court chambers and also was the first office location for many professionals arriving in town, like doctors William A. Davison and C.T. Dixon. It served as home for other transient professionals, like early school teacher W.S. Dawson. The hotel was the incubator for the second newspaper in town, the *Jefferson Inquirer*, and a book binding business. Additionally, it was a public gathering place for dances, dinners, political rallies, and club meetings, such as an early Jockey Club.

The earliest landlord may have been Henry Dixon, or "Uncle Hal," who was host to a public dinner and ball to celebrate Independence Day in 1837. Born in North Carolina, Dixon married Nancy Bolton and moved to Jefferson City in 1832. An iconic triangle bell called people to dinner from the old City Hotel's front porch.

Harrison Rea took over management in August 1838, noting that the hotel was constructed for entertainment as well as comfort. Rea soon left to open his own White House.

The southern line of the eastern and western stages met at the old City Hotel by 1840, when Pennsylvanian William C. Young was keeping the "large and commodious brick" hotel. Future hotelier William H. Ferguson kept the hotel's stable with two carriages, a driver, and livery.

St. George Tucker took over management in the fall of 1842, coming from the Mansion House in Fulton. With only weeks to prepare for the next General Assembly, Tucker was competing with Coulter at the White House, Crump & Jackson at the Missouri House, Newman at the National Hotel, and Basye at the Rising Sun. "Our active and attentive tavern keepers will be fully prepared to meet any calls," the *Jefferson Inquirer* said. Further, "the taverns will not afford the only accommodations: many private families are making preparations to board and lodge members."

Like many hotel operators in the early years of the capital, Tucker lasted less than a biennial season. Born in Virginia, Tucker owned eighty acres in Callaway County, where he returned as tavern keeper.

R.L. Fant took over the old City Hotel in May 1845, preparing the location "on an elevated and healthy spot" with new furniture and bedding.

When local volunteers returned from the Mexican-American War in 1847, William Gunsaullus, former sheriff and then proprietor of City Hotel, served a dinner for returning Jefferson Citians.

Seminary

By the fall of 1849, the hotel was being used as a school rather than a hotel. The name City Hotel was transferred to the northwest corner of Madison and High Streets soon afterward.

Mrs. Buchanan began the Jefferson Female Seminary in 1849 in what was still a large and elegant building. Renovations allowed for the accommodation of many pupils, the windows created air circulation, the school room was spacious, and fireplaces would keep it comfortable in winter. The next year, Mrs. Vanover opened a permanent school there, with attention primarily to moral and mental training of young ladies.

This building came down about 1862. Its replacement eventually housed Mrs. Howe's Boarding House and the Neef Hotel.

Newman's City Hotel

circa 1836–1865

For seventy years, the iconic northwest corner at Madison and High Streets was hotel, gathering place, retail space, and dramatic backdrop to the frequent community events uptown. First the Newman National Hotel, it also went by the Marshall House, the Paulsel House, and finally the Newman's City Hotel. It was not the only location called National Hotel, nor was it the only City Hotel.

It became a landmark, used by surrounding businesses to advertise their location, such as Christopher Wagner's City Bakery, next door on High Street; Flemming and Thompson's building and marble shop across High Street; and the Obermayer brothers store across Madison Street.

National Hotel

Michael Newman, a Virginian, had fitted up a brick building as the National Hotel some time before 1840, when it already was a "well-known establishment." Brothers Thomas Miller and Philip Miller built a house and store on this corner in about 1836. As merchants and land speculators, the Millers likely sold the corner in 1840 to help pay their debts, for which they had been previously imprisoned and declared for bankruptcy in 1842.

The Newman's National Hotel housed the office for the eastern stagecoach's northern line by 1840 and had its own stable, which was set afire in February 1842 at the same time as Harrison Rea's White House. Mayor John F. Hogel put up a $300 reward for the "peaceful and quiet city has for some time past been kept in constant excitement and alarm by some incendiary or incendiaries, setting fire to our property."

By 1844, Michael's son, Hardin Newman, was leasing the National where U.S. Senator Thomas Hart Benton, as well as twenty members of the General Assembly, stayed that fall. "He has good rooms, well furnished, and faithful and attentive servants, indeed everything to make the sojourn of travelers and boarders agreeable, which the western country affords," the *State Sentinel* said.

However, property owners Henry Paulsel and Michael Newman lost the buildings, property, and improvements in a lawsuit brought by the Millers in 1845. They were brothers-in-law, Paulsel having married Newman's sister, Catherine (Newman), in 1825 in Virginia.

Marshall House

John D. Curry took over operations of the corner hotel in the fall of 1846, renaming it the Marshall House. Of Curry, the *Missouri State Times* said that "a more attentive, urbane and accommodating landlord is not to be found."

Curry's wife, Patsy (Hughes), was sister to Burr McCarty's wife, Elzira. They arrived from Virginia in Jefferson City in 1837 on the night of the capitol fire. In the decade before Curry entered the hotel business, he was elected twice as a city aldermen and was on the executive board of the Bible Society of Cole County.

Paulsel House

When Curry left the Marshall House for the Virginia Hotel, Paulsel renamed the corner hotel as the Paulsel House, again making repairs and alterations.

Thomas Jefferson Wilburn moved his tailoring business into the Marshall House in about November 1846. In December 1848, he and his wife, Elizabeth Ann (Gordon), were hired as landlords of the Paulsel House. Wilburn made his own improvements to the large, commodious brick house. The *Weekly Jefferson Inquirer* described him as "an attentive and accommodating landlord and Mrs. Wilburn can't be surpassed as a landlady."

Like so many others, Wilburn had moved from Virginia to Jefferson City by 1832. Wilburn operated a dry goods store and was active in the community, including planning annual Independence Day celebration activities and in development of the local Masonic Temple.

Wilburn's father-in-law and hotelier, John Churchill Gordon Jr., was among the Jefferson Citians who headed to California in the 1849 gold rush. The Wilburns followed in 1854, taking twenty wagons loaded with merchandise to Salt Lake City and a large number of cattle.

Henry Paulsel

Paulsel was among the seventy-six men from Cole County who were first recruited in May 1846 to serve in the Mexican-American War. When the local militia organized in 1845, the battalion muster grounds were located on Paulsel's farm.

The volunteers headed to Mexico were treated to a sumptuous dinner at the Marshall House in May 1846, served by Curry. The company departed aboard the *Linn*. As they left, a German band played and artillery was discharged from Capitol Hill.

Paulsel was discharged at Santa Fe due to rheumatism and arrived back in the Capital City in early November 1846. He reported that they faced measles and mumps outbreaks shortly before he left, although no one from Cole County had yet died. They faced a storm crossing the plains and fought with the Pawnees and Comanches. They also had scarce provisions, forcing them to live on sheep and goat.

Upon the return of the local regiment, another dinner was held, and Paulsel was a main speaker along with officers William Angney, John Walker, and Alex Irvin.

Paulsel was one of two known residents to die in April 1849 of cholera. The local Masonic Lodge resolution noted, "Masonry has lost one of her most accomplished votaries…the community a valuable citizen, ever ready in acts of benevolence to contribute to the wants and necessities of those around him."

After his death, Catherine operated a boarding house in Leavenworth, Kansas. Then she moved to San Francisco, California, where she married Dr. Hawthorne and moved to Portland, Oregon, "immensely wealthy."

Newman's City Hotel

Hardin Newman had applied the new name of Newman's City Hotel by September 1850. His ad said that he was "thankful for past favors" and that he had thoroughly repaired the building and replaced the furniture. After the loss of the family business in 1845, Hardin Newman operated the Newman Boarding House in St. Louis.

Hardin's mother, Rebecca (Smith), was hostess at City Hotel for many years, even after Michael's death in 1852. She "never had an enemy," and "everybody was her friend…she had an extensive acquaintance all over the state, and was remembered by all who were her guests for her kind and hospitable entertainment. All her life she was remarkable for her energy,

A hotel opened in about 1840 at the northwest corner of Madison and High Streets. In 1850, it became the Newman's City Hotel, as seen in this 1859 lithograph by Eduard Robyn. *Brooks Collection.*

perseverance and power of endurance," her 1874 obituary said. To reflect her appeal, her pallbearers included seven-time mayor Captain Jefferson T. Rogers, former state adjutant general James L. Minor, and attorney James B. McHenry.

In August 1858, Hardin Newman built the largest building in Tipton, the Prairie House hotel, and sent his City Hotel manager, Fred Hepp, to operate it. Hardin was part of organizing the First Annual Fair of the Cole County Agricultural and Mechanical Association in the fall of 1860. At the same time, he was on the local committee to receive the Honorable Stephen A. Douglas prior to the November 1860 presidential election.

However, during the Civil War, Hardin was arrested in October 1862 for "giving aid and comfort to the enemy." By November 1865, Newman had returned to St. Louis, operating the Clarendon Hotel with L.F. Garner near the Pacific Railroad depot.

In August 1861, future general Ulysses S. Grant was stationed in Jefferson City. Local lore says his headquarters was at the City Hotel.

During the Civil War, Southern sympathizers were known to congregate at the City Hotel, including Judge William C. Young, Dr. Robert Young, Sheriff Green C. Berry, Judge Gustavus A. Parsons, Judge William E. Dunscombe, ferryman Jefferson T. Rogers, and hotelier Burr McCarty.

Two famous engravings by George Caleb Bingham hung on the walls of the City Hotel, not only before the war but also for forty years afterward—the 1852 *County Election* and 1853 *Stump Speaking*.

WHITE HOUSE

For the traveling public along Missouri's frontier, taverns could provide both sustenance and beds. These accommodations were essential for the young capital. The Callaway County Ramsey family were involved from day one in the formation of Jefferson City. Not surprisingly, they were among the earliest such tavern keepers.

Ramsey's Tavern sat on Main Street "in front of the Capitol and lower steamboat landing" before 1834.

Harrison Rea converted the brick saloon into the White House in August 1838 after working for two years at the old City Hotel. Rea's "urbanity of manners and experience in the business, make him peculiarly well qualified for a landlord," the newspapers said.

In March 1842, an incendiary device took down Rea's White House. Although Mayor John F. Hogel made a proclamation with a $300 reward to find the villain, Rea moved to Davies County.

The hotel was restored before the next General Assembly by George W. Coulter. With a livery attached and attentive servants, the White House was considered large for its time with comfortable beds and convenience to the capitol. When Thomas Hart Benton visited the city in 1840 and 1842, he chose to stay at the White House.

As often happened at local hotels, curiosities were put on display. In early 1843, one was a large tooth found in Benton County, "a species of animals at some former period of the world, inhabiting this country, compared with which, all now in existence are mere pigmys."

Keeping hotels in the earliest days of the Capital City was hard going. Coulter filed for bankruptcy in February 1843.

McCarty House

1838–1906

Virginia horse master Burr Harrison McCarty found Jefferson City in need of a livery when he arrived in 1836. McCarty then drove the mail wagon for fellow Virginian Thomas Lawson Price, who had the U.S. Mail contract.

A congenial and generous fellow, McCarty was quick to strike up conversations with the few passengers he could carry on his route. He often invited the travelers coming to Jefferson City to stay at his home, on the south side of Van Buren Street (future McCarty Street). Eventually, McCarty owned the entire block, which included his livery and slave quarters.

In 1844, McCarty and his wife, Elzira (Hughes), made an addition to their house, built by workers already in town working on the second capitol, adding accommodations for up to sixteen boarders. As was the custom of the day, the rooms had no locks. Even when county sheriffs and collectors brought in loads of coin for the state treasurer, seldom was there a robbery.

Here he built the city's first livery, feed, and stable in 1841 and maintained it as the "most excellent outside St. Louis" for more than thirty years. His stable at the southeast corner of Jefferson and McCarty Streets was brick, well ventilated, and designed for natural light. Because it was built below street level, it was uniquely cooler in summer and warmer in winter. It was ninety by thirty-five feet, allowing room for more than thirty-two stalls and fifteen buggies. A horseman by trade, he kept fine harness and saddle horses. The ground floor opened to an acre lot and the second to street level. This main floor held the office, a sleeping room, and a harness closet. The third floor was a loft, storing up to thirty tons of hay.

Burr Harrison McCarty opened the McCarty House in 1838. *Henry Gensky.*

Before his retirement in 1881, McCarty also brought the first two omnibuses to Jefferson City, purchased from New York.

McCarty's early influence is apparent when, in 1854, the city aldermen granted his request to rename Van Buren Street to McCarty Street. According to historian Henry Gensky, McCarty was angered by the former president's alignment with antislavery factions of the Democratic Party.

Home-Style Meals

Its southern-style meals and clean and cozy surroundings, made possible by its enslaved women, made the McCarty House a popular stop for nearly a century.

Familiar comforts of Virginia, such as a pot of coffee and fresh-baked cornbread, were prepared by Cassandra "Cassie" Crump, who reigned in the McCarty kitchen from 1837 to 1876.

Crump was about twenty years old when she was brought from Virginia by Elzira McCarty. Crump's obituary said that her "art did so much to give McCarty's hotel a widespread reputation for the excellence of its tables." Never to be called "Cassie McCarty," Crump "put plenty of whisky in the mincemeat and an abundance of rum in the punch," the *Kansas City Star* reported.

Mary Stokes, born enslaved in Callaway County, apprenticed under Crump and took over, working for forty-seven years in the McCarty kitchen. Stokes continued with diligent attention to the old-fashioned recipes, including breakfast biscuits and cornbread for dinner. She was unwilling to leave her kitchen to anyone else, even when offered retirement with full pay.

During the 1904 Democratic convention held in Jefferson City, four newspapermen sent for meals from the McCarty House kitchen. So surprised at their meal, they later visited the hotel, and each gave Stokes a silver dollar as a tip of appreciation for her skill in the kitchen.

Stokes was aided by Mary Jackson, called "Jack," who was head waiter. "Every judge of the Missouri Supreme Court and every governor the state has had since Silas Woodson was the executive has been proud to claim an acquaintance with Jack," the *Kansas City Star* reported.

Stokes and Jackson continued to live in the old cabin behind the hotel for twenty-eight years after emancipation. Jack reared Joshua, Bob, and Sallie, who worked at the hotel and learned to play cards from a Supreme Court judge. Stokes' son, Robert Wyatt, went on to become a world traveler and operated the Silver Moon Hotel at 209 Monroe Street.

Civil War

Not shy about their southern views, Burr and Elzira McCarty were said to have refused to fly the Stars and Stripes or house Union officers who sought quarters there.

Before General John Frémont's troops arrived September 26, 1861, as many as twenty journalists from the East had gathered in Jefferson City because Missouri had the only wartime action at the time. It was the largest gathering of journalists since the Battle of Bull Run, including Albert Richardson of the *New York Tribune*, Thomas Knox of the *New York Herald*, Richard Colburn of the *New York World*, Alex Simplot of *Harper's Weekly*, and Henri Lovie of *Frank Leslie's Illustrated.*

They all stayed at the McCarty House, which Richardson described as "a wretched little tavern." Here they adopted the name "Bohemian Brigade." The term became synonymous with "war correspondent" by the end of the Civil War and was continued in use for several other conflicts for the embedded journalists.

Junius Henri Browne from the *New York Tribune* said that they had "taken quarters in an ancient hotel, a rambling structure built on several levels around a courtyard with wide galleries in the rear. The place was run by a courtly old gentleman with a white goatee."

When Confederate General Sterling Price made his 1864 raid, the hotel was barricaded and holes made in its brick walls for rifle fire. After the fall skirmishes, the hotel, like other homes and churches, served as a hospital.

Politics

The McCarty House was the political headquarters of many camps over the years, including that of Thomas Hart Benton. It was the preferred hotel of many of the state's prominent dignitaries, including Governor John Phelps and U.S. Senator Francis Cockrell. When the present Governor's Mansion was being erected, Governor B. Gratz Brown took his residence there.

U.S. District Judge John Phillips credited the McCarty House with "unbounded hospitality, home like simplicity and unsurpassed table." Of the hotel's founder, he recalled a man "bright with wit and stinging with sarcasm in the midst of interchange of repartee and discussion of leading men."

Burr McCarty's grandson, Wilbur Lee McCarty, remembered the house as a "lounging place of political fixers and home of caucuses" and his grandfather as a "natural host and storyteller." Dr. Robert Young called McCarty "one of the most notable characters who ever lived in Jefferson City."

The front room of the Old McCarty House was part of the original home and served as the office, where the original mantel and fireplace remained throughout its seventy years. "In the office there is still the old-

The McCarty House stood from 1838 to 1965 on the south side of McCarty Street between Jefferson and McCarty. *Missouri State Archives.*

time inn suggestion of warmth and good cheer, a fireplace in which the dry wood crackles and sends its embers up the chimney and its light out in the darkened room," Harry Norman wrote for the *St. Louis Republic*.

As other hotels continually added modern conveniences, the McCarty House retained its nineteenth-century charm. Only gas lighting to replace candles was added and that only after McCarty's death. However, McCarty's hotel was the first to include a marble-topped bureau.

The twenty rooms had downy feather beds, the place was always clean and tidy, and the kitchen was renowned beyond Missouri's borders. "The table was always the best in the city and the house always filled to capacity," the *St. Louis Globe-Democrat* wrote at its closing in 1906.

When the old yellow building came down in 1965 to make way for what is today Legends Bank, it was one of the three oldest buildings still standing—the others being Lohman's Landing and the Parsons House on Jackson Street.

Ella McCarty

After McCarty's death in 1890, his eldest daughter, Ella, continued the old-fashioned hotel for another sixteen years. Then it was transformed into apartments and, later, a retail space.

Ella McCarty had attended Jefferson Female College, with classmates including Maria and Mary Jefferson, Cornelia Wells, and Nannie Minor. She was a member of "society," attending balls in fanciful gowns and having her name listed in many newspaper accounts of the most elite parties in the city.

She was equally impressive as a hotelier. Ella McCarty shared her father's knack for "unbounded hospitality [and] home-like simplicity," and she was full of common sense and assuredness in the way things should be done.

Newspaperman John Edwards, who negotiated the surrender of Frank James to Governor Thomas Crittenden, died in 1889 in his bed at the McCarty House. His death "created a profound sensation throughout the city," a newspaper reported. A funeral procession, led by Governor David Francis, followed from the hotel to the train station. And Ella, who was good friends with Mrs. Edwards, accompanied her.

Like her father, Ella did not fly the American flag over the McCarty House until 1898, after the battleship *Maine* exploded in a Cuban harbor. This incident, among others, spurred Congress to declare war against Spain and call five thousand soldiers from Missouri into the Spanish-American War. Former Union officer and frontier soldier Nelson Cole, who became a brigadier general in the U.S. Army, was a good friend of the McCarty family. Ella McCarty made a personal appeal to Governor Lon Stephens to make Cole's appointment to the state militia. When Stephens called Ella McCarty personally to confirm, she raised the Stars and Stripes above the old hotel. "This news was enough to shake the Capitol to its very foundation stone, and the flag-raising was one of the events of that year," the *St. Louis Republican* said.

Of Ella McCarty, Congressman and Judge John Phillips said, "Although misfortunes, at time, seemed to be enamored of her parts; although burdens and struggles accumulated as the seasons came and went, she never failed to rise to the emergent occasion. With unyielding fortitude, wise discretion and a brave heart, she seemed to possess the alchemy of transmuting disasters into good fortune."

First Missouri House

circa 1840–circa 1859

Essential to the arrival of elected officials, as well as most visitors to the Capital City before 1855, was the city landing at the north end of Jefferson Street. Here was the heart of the city's early commercial development.

The first Missouri House opened in about 1840 in the upper two floors of the iconic three-story stone building known today as Lohman's Landing. The building was built in three sections around 1836, likely by either contractor Henry Colgan or stonemason James Crump. When complete, it was the largest building in the city, even taller than the 1826 statehouse.

James Crump

James Alvin Crump bought the Greek Revival building in 1838, soon after the site was designated for a fifteen-year contract from the General Assembly to keep a ferry across the Missouri River to the mouth of Cedar Creek.

Born in Kentucky, Crump moved from Callaway County to Jefferson City. Crump was a varied entrepreneur, involved in investments, blacksmithing,

The Missouri House was opened in about 1840 at the city landing, and in 1842, a portico was added across the front, as seen in this 1859 lithograph by Eduard Robyn. *Brooks Collection.*

stone cutting, tavern keeping, ferry operations, real estate, and general construction. As a builder, Crump was involved in the first Cole County Courthouse in Jefferson City, the old stone church on Main Street, and the original stonework at the Missouri State Penitentiary.

Crump opened a grocery store in the west section of the wharf building, carrying hardware, shoes, liquor, and other items important to travelers. In 1840, he sold the center section to Enos Basye Cordell and James Dunnica, who ran a freight and warehouse business, because river packets and commercial steamers did not have port storage facilities early on in steamboat operations. The east section was a tavern kept by John Yount.

A portico extending the length of the front was added in the fall of 1842. At the same time, Crump bought back the rest of the building and took on partner Richard Belt Jackson. Born to English immigrants in Maryland, Jackson moved to Kentucky by 1812 and to Auxvasse by 1831, where he soon was elected justice of the peace. He was a commissioner of the permanent seat of government and served as doorkeeper of the House of Representatives from 1834 until his death in 1855.

James Herndon

The Missouri House passed from Crump to Cordell in October 1843. Cordell leased hotel operations to James F. Herndon, who was city collector at the time. Immediately, Herndon set to making improvements to "make it without a doubt one of the largest and best hotels on the river," a *State Sentinel* ad said. The basement bar was "always supplied with all kinds of choice wines, liquors and cigars."

With a reputation already in place, Herndon added his interests in hunting and fishing and his skill as a cook to improve the riverside tavern. In the spring of 1848, he joined entrepreneurs from other small communities along the Missouri to provide a comfortable passenger packet, the *St. Louis Oak*, weekly from St. Louis to Boonville and back.

Cholera

Herndon left the Missouri House in September 1849 to farm in Callaway County. Earlier that fateful year, the *Steamer Monroe* had arrived with a cholera epidemic. A scathing letter to the St. Louis newspaper *Reveille* accused Herndon by name of poorly treating these travelers. The few survivors later refuted the earlier letter, but the toll may have been too much.

Cordell also closed his "long and honorable mercantile" business at this location following his personal losses to the epidemic, including his wife, an infant son, a teenage daughter, and a promising brother.

Archibald Cearnal

Archibald W. Cearnal Jr. next operated the Missouri House. A half brother of the Boltons and nephew to the Dixons, Cearnal was well connected with the early landowners in Cole County. Born in North Carolina, his mother, Mary Polly (Dixon), was the widow of William Bolton when she married Cearnal's father. Cearnal moved with his mother, maternal grandmother

This daguerreotype by Thomas Easterly dated 1850 shows the Stone Warehouse, occupied by Charles Lohman. *Missouri Historical Society.*

Catherine (Warren Dixon), and older Bolton stepbrothers to Missouri in about 1832. Cearnal invested in steamboats for trade, was a freight agent for several packets, and rented enslaved men to work on the boats.

Pacific Railroad Hotel

Reflecting the anticipation of the town's future railroad stop, the hotel's name in May 1853 became the Pacific Railroad Hotel. Owners George Lansdown and Sampson Diuguid Patteson refitted with new furniture. "It would seem they are striving industriously to merit the patronage of the traveling community," the *Jefferson Inquirer* said.

Lansdown was a construction painter from Virginia and supported three unmarried sisters. Previously, Lansdown operated the barroom of the Virginia Hotel, two blocks south on Jefferson Street, serving brandies, wines, cigars, oysters, sardines, lobster, clams, cheese, and crackers.

Lansdown died in July 1854 at age thirty-six, leaving Patteson the sole named proprietor for both the commission and forwarding business, as well as the Pacific Hotel, which had dropped "Railroad" from its name.

Also a Virginian, Patteson previously operated stagecoaches and mail delivery from St. Louis to Fulton.

Tilford's Pacific Hotel

The gentlemanly William Hume Tilford was operating the landing hotel as Tilford's Pacific Hotel in 1856. Tilford also operated a grocery store on High Street that featured the new technology of a soda fountain. He did not stay long and may have left under unscrupulous circumstances.

St. Charles Hotel

August Foss took over the now St. Charles Hotel in December 1856. The newspaper assured travelers that "the accommodating host and his estimable lady, will make their house a pleasant place of sojourn for the weary traveler." George Washington Capell, formerly of the *Steamboat Genoa*, was in charge of the barroom.

St. Louis Hotel

The St. Louis Hotel name replaced "St. Charles" in May 1858, when New York–born Capell advanced as proprietor. The *Missouri State Times* described Capell as a "very clever gentleman." However, Capell was only here a year, failing to repay a loan.

In May 1859, the property was sold to the highest bidder, including the following items: twenty-three double beds, fifteen single beds, seventy-eight dining room and bedroom chairs, five long dining room tables, three wire safes, eleven carpets, fifteen washstands/bowls/pitchers, eight room tables, eleven looking glasses, eight stoves and pipes, and two ice chests.

The building became tenements and warehouses for the next forty years, until the Tweedie Footwear Corporation took over the buildings. The building was restored in 1976 and is maintained by the Missouri Department of Natural Resources.

Part III

1841 to 1854

A poem published in an 1841 *Weekly Jefferson Inquirer* praised four of the local hotels:

On rising ground, from all sides round;
And near the state house too,
The City Hotel, with triangle bell,
Presents its front to view.

And just below, towards river's shore;
Where steam boats land in sight,
A street called main to entertain,
There stands the house call White.

Another Hotel, supplied as well,
On corner where two streets cross
Presents to view, two sides most new
And Newman is the boss.

One more stand I have on hand;
The sign is Rising Sun
It stands on shore, not far below;
And now of inns I'm done.

Mexican-American War

The war with Mexico appealed to most mid-Missourians—either as southern sympathizers, pioneers, or capitalists—so, the county sent two hundred men in the summer of 1846; thirty did not return.

When the call for troops was announced, the community held a meeting at the courthouse led by General Gustavus Parsons. Hotelier Andreas Sachs was among eight leaders called to make addresses, as was hotelier and druggist Tennessee Mathews.

While waiting to head west to Fort Leavenworth, the local recruits trained at the farm of hotelier Henry Paulsel, who was among them. Also among these volunteers was hotelier William Ferguson, who was wounded at the Battle of Taos. Before they left town for Santa Fe, hotelier John Curry treated them to a meal at his Marshall House.

By the fall of 1846, Paulsel had been sent home from Santa Fe due to rheumatism. However, he was able to relay many stories, funds, and letters to loved ones at home. For example, they met a snowstorm crossing the plains and encountered trouble with the Pawnees and Comanches on the trail.

Sachs and Curry were joined by hotelier William Kerr on the committee to superintend artillery salutes from Capitol Hill to celebrate victories in the field. And when the Cole County volunteers returned in July 1847, Curry led the welcoming committee, organizing a barbecue.

Many of the soldiers who had gone to Mexico left again following the California Gold Rush. Dozens left Cole County for short term or for life, including Gordon, Sachs' brother, Curry's son, and Wilburn.

The 1850s were the "golden era" of steam boating along the Missouri River, with as many as sixty packets and another forty boats plying the muddy waters. But its greatest competition also emerged in 1849 with a movement to build a rail line west from St. Louis called the Pacific Railroad, which reached Jefferson City in 1856.

At the beginning of the 1842 General Assembly session, a directory of elected officials showed sixteen boarding at the Missouri House. The old City Hotel kept thirteen and seven at the White House. Only four boarded at the Rising Sun, three at McCarty's, and three at Newman's National Hotel. Another fourteen stayed at "Colonel Price's," and George W. Miller entertained nine General Assembly members. "Our active and attentive tavern keepers will be fully prepared to meet any calls," the *Inquirer* said.

FERGUSON HOUSE

1844–1875

William H. Ferguson and his wife, Zerelda (Lansdown), opened a boarding house at 225 West High Street. His rooms boasted carpet and excellent fireplaces. At least ten legislators for the 1844–45 session chose the Rural Choice Boarding House at the southeast corner of Broadway and High Street. A short walk to the capitol, it was next door to Mrs. Obermayer's boarding house and opposite the Catholic convent.

In 1859, Ferguson built a new brick house at the same location but changed the name to the Ferguson House. It was furnished with fine style

William Ferguson opened the Rural Choice Boarding House in 1844 and then built a brick house on the same corner of Broadway and High Street in 1859, renaming it the Ferguson House, as seen in this 1859 lithograph by Eduard Robyn. *Brooks Collection.*

and large rooms. Ferguson sold the property in 1865 and then opened another Ferguson House in Kansas City.

Floyd Crandall bought the property, and the Zumwalt brothers managed the Ferguson House into the late 1860s.

Indiana House

Locals began calling it the Indiana House after Indiana Bolton took over management of the popular but modest hotel. Bolton was born in Osage Township, daughter of Meriweather and Sadie (Hall) Bolton.

The Indiana House fell to fire in March 1875. Next door, Moritz Obermayer's woodshed caught fire, which spread to his "beautiful" twenty-year-old home and ultimately claimed the small hotel next door. All the families and boarders, including Bolton's father, were saved.

The city fire company experienced several mishaps during the 4:00 a.m. winter fire, including a burst hose. The *State Journal* reported that the "brick melted like wood." Although they had time to save a little of the furniture and clothing, Indiana Bolton did not have insurance on the furniture.

Judge Arnold Krekel bought both the Indiana House and the Obermayer's lots in the fall and contracted with Fred Binder to build a home on the remains.

After her father died in 1876, Indiana Bolton moved near Fort Benton, Montana, where she kept a hotel and then married English rancher Thomas Coatsworth in the fall of 1877.

SACHS-WAGNER HOUSE

circa 1846–circa 1892

Andreas Sachs opened a boarding house "on High Street a few doors west of the corner of High and Madison streets" before November 1846. This became known as the (second) National Hotel after the name was no longer associated with what became the Marshall House.

Sachs arrived in Jefferson City before 1845, having lived in St. Charles for at least a decade. Politically, he was a Thomas Hart Benton supporter, and in the spring of 1848, he was elected as a Democrat to the city's board of aldermen. When the convention was called in St. Louis in the fall of 1849 to see the completion of the Central Pacific Railroad, Sachs was sent as a delegate.

Charles Feyerlein, who had operated the (first) Missouri House at the city landing, bought this (second) National Hotel about 1854. He advertised not only the hotel but also the bar, bakery, and dining room with the motto "Friendly reception and prompt attention." In March 1857, John Schott & Company advertised splendid lunches served at the (second) National Hotel.

Wagner Hotel

Paulus Wagner bought the property in December 1859, renaming it the Wagner Hotel. O. Herman Petschow was in charge of the hotel and the Oyster Saloon and Restaurant.

Born in Germany, Petschow and his wife, Theresa, arrived in Jefferson City by 1858, the same year he and John Opel opened the Flower Garden restaurant and walking garden. A passenger wagon ran from Opel's house every Sunday to the garden, where they served ice cream, oysters, sardines, beefsteak, veal steak, ham, eggs, pigeons, chickens, cheese, lager beer, lemonade, coffee, and chocolate.

Of Petschow's Oyster Saloon, the *Weekly Jefferson Inquirer* said, "Strangers will find this one of the best institutions of its kind in the state" and Petschow a "perfect connoisseur."

At the beginning of the Civil War, the Wagner house boarded officers of the Second Missouri Volunteer, while Petschow served as a lieutenant in John Peasner's Company A of the Cole County Home Guard. Later in the war, Petschow requested an appointment in the Secret Service or to be an assistant provost marshal. However, General Thomas Lawson Price and other state officials voiced their concerns, describing him as prying, meddlesome, mischievous, unscrupulous, and dishonest.

As things settled following the Civil War, the German association of Turners held a New Year's celebration at the Wagner Hotel to kick off 1866. Petschow followed up with a masquerade ball on February 1. "Petschow can beat the world in managing an affair of this kind," the *Jefferson City Tribune* said.

Next, a ladies' ice cream saloon was opened in the Wagner Hotel's front parlor, and Petschow reopened the Jefferson City Oyster Depot with his reputation for knowing how to cook them. But the contents of the hotel were sold at a sheriff's sale to pay Petschow's debt in the fall of 1867.

Fresh Oyster Phenomenon

One of the more surprising long-term trends in the hotel kitchens and uptown restaurants was the proud promotion of the availability of fresh oysters. This was not isolated to Jefferson City but rather was a Midwestern craze as harvesting, preserving, and transporting technologies improved.

Because of their abundance in the nineteenth century, oysters were lower in cost than other proteins of the time. Even before the first insulated railroad boxcars arrived, oysters captured in ice blocks and insulated with straw were transported by steamboat. Menus could include fried oysters, broiled oysters, stewed oysters, escalloped oysters, fricasseed oysters, pickled oysters, oyster croquettes, oyster patties, oyster pie, oyster soup, or oyster toast.

The earliest local mention of fresh oysters was 1851 at Henry Cordell's saloon on the city wharf. Within the year, George Lansdown had added the same to his Virginia Hotel barroom. "It is quite a treat in our little city to enjoy the taste of good fresh oysters," the *Inquirer* said.

Charles Eckler was advertising fresh oysters prepared in any style at his Veranda Saloon on the southwest corner of High and Madison Streets by 1855. Then the Capitol Oyster Saloon opened soon after near the southwest corner of High and Jefferson Streets, Charles Feyerlein's Oyster Saloon opened at a corner of Washington and High Streets, and Davis' Restaurant and Game Depot advertised "choice oysters" at its Jefferson Street location.

Just before the Civil War, Herman Petschow opened his Oyster Saloon and Restaurant in the Wagner Hotel. The *Inquirer* called him a "perfect connoisseur" with a reputation of knowing how to prepare oysters. After the war, Petschow reopened as the Jefferson City Oyster Depot, paired with a ladies' ice cream saloon on High Street.

While dedicated restaurants faded in the following decades, oysters remained a common pairing at saloons. Banquets and community Thanksgiving dinner menus of the 1880s were not complete without a few oyster dishes. Even as late as 1907, the improved Hotel Madison promoted its new café featuring fresh oysters and lobster.

Successful tinsmith and hotel operator Herman Neef took charge of the Wagner Hotel in the summer of 1876, leaving behind his self-named boarding house on Madison Street.

In 1892, George Wagner improved the front entrance of the then "Old" Wagner Hotel for other commercial pursuits.

VIRGINIA HOUSE

1848–1969

By far the wealthiest man in the Capital City, Thomas Lawson Price built his polished stone mansion on an advantageous hill just south of the capitol in 1841. Through the 1840s, dozens of legislators and prominent visitors stayed in his Colonial-style home, by far the largest in town. It featured wrought-iron verandas on each side and a white columned double gallery across the front.

The home was taken down in 1905 and replaced by the current Supreme Court building. The stone was reused to build the Bassman House in the 200 block of West McCarty Street, which was razed by the city in 2007. Some of the Price Mansion's luxurious original furnishings are on display at the Cole County Historical Society museum.

The Price Mansion was a traditional location for balls, receptions, and parties. According to Capitol Historian Bob Priddy, it was the site of "an unbroken custom for many years for the incoming governor and his wife to be received first at the Price home."

Thomas Lawson Price

When Price was just twenty, he inherited his father's Virginia tobacco plantation, the enslaved people, and the family reputation dating back to the 1600s. Two years later, he moved to Missouri with his wife, Lydia (Bolton), his sister, his in-laws, and nearly forty enslaved people. With the onset of the second cholera pandemic in St. Louis in 1832, they moved on to Jefferson City, where several Boltons and other family friends already had settled.

Price first opened a mercantile and made smart investments in real estate. In 1838, he received the federal mail contract between St. Louis and Jefferson City, and he then began the first Jefferson City–St. Louis stage line with Burr McCarty. When Jefferson City officially incorporated in 1839, he was its first mayor, serving two terms. By 1870, he owned a combined $1 million (nearly $32 million in 2025 dollars) in personal property and real estate.

Active in politics, Price befriended generations of judges, governors, and other officials through his growing presence in Jefferson City. He was defeated for state treasurer in 1838 and for state senate in 1845. He was elected lieutenant governor in 1849 and as Cole County's representative in 1860. He lost a bid for governor in 1864 but then served as vice-president of the Democratic National Convention in 1868 in New York.

As recorded in Goodspeed's *History of Cole County*, Price was remembered as an "able political debater, subsequently proving himself a clear, forcible and logical speaker; ready at repartee, abounding in useful information and fully imbued with the spirit and principles of [the Democratic Party]."

He was both firmly pro-Union and a vocal supporter of legal slavery. Price was president of the Jefferson City Land Company, which in 1855 intended to bring free white labor to Central Missouri, considering "slave society in Mid-Missouri an economic handicap."

"He was but one of many Virginians who came to Missouri in the early days, but his career is outstanding in the annals of Missouri history," Missouri historian Floyd Shoemaker said.

Virginia Hotel

In November 1848, Price built the Virginia Hotel with convict labor, superintended by William C. Young. The large brick structure stood "pleasantly and conveniently" on High Street at the northwest corner with Jefferson Street. It featured twenty-four large, well-finished rooms.

The first landlord was Billy Crawford. By 1849, John and Patsy Curry had left the Marshall House to operate the Virginia Hotel. Within a few months, Curry added a bar to the basement, stocked with the finest liquors from the St. Louis markets.

The Virginia House was opened in 1848 at the northwest corner of Jefferson and High Streets. This is how it looked in 1891, when sketched by Frederick Suden. *Missouri State Archives.*

William Kerr

When the Currys opened the Jefferson House catty-corner from the Virginia Hotel in 1852, William Dillon Kerr took over until 1863. In addition to his hotel work, he was elected sheriff for eight years and served as U.S. marshal for eleven years. At his death in 1876, he had been city registrar for several years.

Born in Virginia, Kerr came to Jefferson City in 1837 by way of Callaway County. In 1845, Kerr married his third wife, Henrietta, daughter of fellow hotel operator Michael Newman. Kerr also was the first superintendent of the state's Deaf and Dumb Asylum in Fulton in 1851.

Shooting

By default, hotels were places to take strangers who needed care, as in the case of Leeper Hale, who was shot on June 15, 1866, the day General Frank P. Blair spoke in Jefferson City. J. Christy Watson had taken over as proprietor of the Virginia Hotel in 1863. It was left to him to care for the wounded Hale.

A mass meeting of Central Missouri Johnson Clubs in the Capital City brought special trains from both sides of the state. Flags were displayed from hotels and homes, and the streets were lively all day. At 2:00 p.m., the local band played. Then Price called the meeting of thousands at the courthouse to order. Blair was stumping for President Andrew Johnson; his focus was on fully incorporating those from the southern cause back into national life and to keep power out of the hands of the "fanatics and abolitionists." At the same time, Stone and Oglesby, who were the radicals, spoke from the capitol steps to about 100 white and 150 Black residents.

That evening, a row occurred at a grog shop, growing out of personal matters and whiskey. The result was the severe shooting of three men. Police were prevented from making an arrest by the other men in the saloon, and the mayor refused to have the place closed.

Daniel Louis died immediately, and Hale's father survived. Hale died of his wounds one month later at the Virginia Hotel.

J. Christy Watson

Missouri-born J. Christy Watson kept the Virginia Hotel from 1863 to 1872, when he was appointed city collector and commissioner of the permanent seat of government. After the Civil War, the Virginia Hotel lost the prestige it once held, and newer hotels like the Madison and Monroe brought stiff competition.

In 1871, the hotel was three stories with a basement, sixty by seventy feet, as well as thirty-five rooms and a good kitchen. Mayor Price's son, Thomas B. Price, began searching for a buyer for the Virginia.

First Jefferson House

1853–1886

A grand home became a prestigious hotel for dignitaries through the middle of the nineteenth century. The Jefferson House set back from the street with a large porch spanning the entire front facing north on High Street.

John Douglas Curry and his wife, Patsy (Hughes), opened their "large and convenient" Jefferson House at 104–106 East High Street in November 1853. Curry previously worked at the Marshall, the City, and the Virginia Hotels.

The Currys moved their young family, including her sister, the future Mrs. Burr McCarty, from Virginia in 1837. Just five years later, John Curry was elected a city alderman for two terms and partnered with George W. Hough as merchants.

Curry helped organize the Bible Society of Cole County Auxiliary in 1846 to circulate English copies and collect donations. Then he was involved in the arrangements for the welcome barbecue for the Cole County Infantry upon its return from Santa Fe in July 1847.

Despite his age, at the beginning of the Civil War, John Curry joined the Third Missouri Volunteers, Company D. But he died in July 1863 at a regimental hospital. Of him, the *Missouri State Times* said that "a more attentive, urbane and accommodating landlord is not to be found…as 'mine host' of the Jefferson House…long and favorably known by visitors to the Capital."

In about 1868, N.W. Parker Sr became proprietor of the Jefferson House. Then Sam Nichols managed it from 1873 to 1874. By 1875, the Jefferson was in the hands of Elias Chambers. And then Patsy Curry returned in 1876 to occupy and reorganize the Jefferson House. The newspaper noted, "The established reputation of this house and the long experience of the present proprietor is a sufficient guarantee to the public that they will here find all the comforts of a first-class hotel."

After Patsy's death in 1884, the property passed to the son Dr. William Curry. Dr. Curry located his medical practice in Jefferson City the summer of 1851 and for a time also was editor of the *State Times*. In 1871, Dr. Curry even partnered with his uncle, Burr McCarty, to operate the Hotel Madison.

At the end of its days, the Jefferson House was sandwiched between two significant business houses on High Street, no longer the single, grand building set back from the corner. It gained a reputation as a "bawdy house." For the last several years, it was boarding for several African American families.

Next door, on the southwest corner of High and Jefferson Streets, Dr. Curry built in 1874 a twenty-five-by-one-hundred-foot, three-story business house. Louis Lohman leased it for his mercantile store and then bought the building in 1883.

In 1886, Lohman bought and razed the historic Jefferson House to fulfill his long-held dream of a local opera house. "This will be a valuable improvement to the city, in addition to getting a building out of the way that has long since become an eye sore," the newspaper of the time said.

PART IV
1855 TO 1860

Anticipating the railroad opening on November 1, 1855, the hoteliers and town were shocked by the Gasconade River Bridge disaster, when the locomotive *O'Sullivan* plunged to its ruin on its maiden voyage. It resulted in the death of thirty-one people, including railroad and city dignitaries.

One year after the Gasconade Bridge disaster, dignitaries from St. Louis again accompanied Pacific Railroad officials on a special train to the Capital City in August 1856. They were entertained at Newman's by the Jeffersonians musical group, followed by speeches by President William McPherson, former mayor Price, and Mayor Jefferson T. Rogers.

The *St. Louis Republican* in the fall of 1856 praised Jefferson City's ingenuity in growing beyond just a company town, limited by its rural location. In particular, it noted that Newman's "City Hotel will sustain the high reputation it has commanded for years by those who have enjoyed its hospitality."

Jefferson City saw a boon in visitors and in commerce. As the westernmost point of the railroad, passengers then boarded steamboats or stagecoaches for other points west. So much demand in this narrow window of time caused the House of Representatives to pass a resolution that the General Assembly be transferred to St. Louis. The House also passed a resolution directing the doorkeeper to prohibit use of the basement committee rooms for sleeping.

In response, the newspaper implored the city's lifeblood to have patience: "Capitalists will not be long in supplying the wants of the public…a hotel would pay a handsome profit."

In 1857, both Dr. Tennessee Mathews and Dr. Bernard Bruns built substantial buildings on High Street. Bruns added a three-story, three-row boarding house, and Mathews built his three-story brick hotel on the south side of the 100 block of East High Street. This same year, the Female Seminary was completed on Water Street, a bridge was installed on the state road in front of the capitol, and the railroad's depot was lit with gas.

"They deserve high commendation for their public spirit and enterprise. They are among the most useful of our citizens. They do not sit down on the shady side of somebody else's house and say a city cannot be built here, 'because it never has been built here before,'" the *Inquirer* said of the doctors.

Two passenger cars arrived and left daily, and six packets left Jefferson City's landing each week. Streets had been improved, schools added, new stores opened, and more buildings were being constructed on High Street. The boom was short-lived, as the rail line reached Tipton in 1858.

NEW PACIFIC HOTEL

circa 1855–after 1953

Bavarian mason John Nicholas Bauer established a cement boarding house and beer saloon at the southwest corner of Monroe and Water Streets as the American House in about 1855. East and across Water Street, today's State Street, was the old Missouri Pacific Depot. Early proprietors included Emma (Colgan) Sanford and Fred Knaup.

From its early days, Bauer's hotel attracted a bit different clientele from the uptown hotels seeking professionals and politicians. Across from the train station, the hotel's saloon was as popular to travelers as the rooms. In addition to travelers, the hotel and saloon were frequented by railroad employees. It also seemed to have a greater exposure to crime.

One April evening in 1872, night engine dispatcher Charles Carby was stabbed to death by his good friend John W. Kile, a locomotive engineer. They had been playing cards when a quarrel grew into an assault. Carby swung a chair and Kile a knife. Witness testimony said that Kile accused Carby of cheating, so Carby hit Kile over the head with a chair. Then Kile took Carby's arm and said something about being friends and not wanting Carby to face the consequences of hitting him again. A fistfight followed in

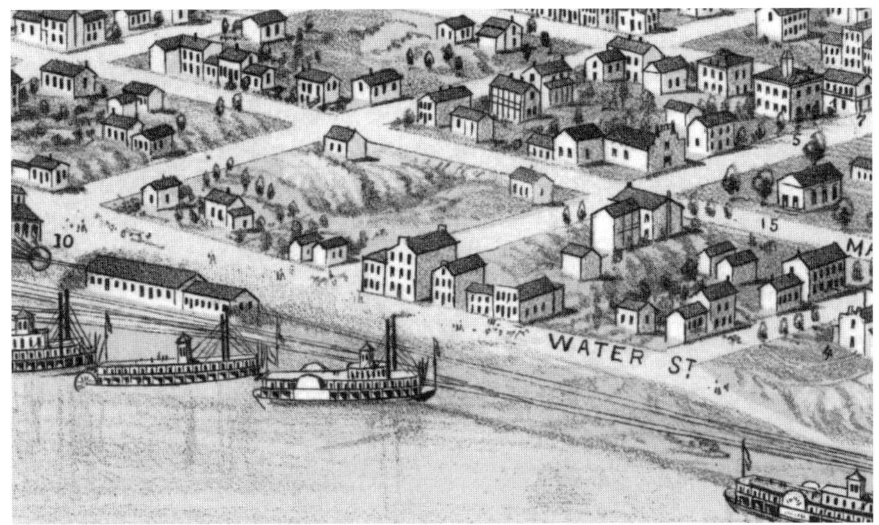

The (second) Pacific Hotel (*center of image*) was in convenient access to the Missouri Pacific Railroad depot. *Library of Congress.*

which Kile stabbed Carby seven times, despite witnesses repeatedly trying to separate the two.

By 1873, Thomas H. Ragg, Bauer's son-in-law, was proprietor. Ragg emigrated from England, married Christina (Bauer), and became a saloon keeper. That allowed Bauer to be more involved in community affairs, such as the Cole County Agricultural and Mechanical Association, First National Bank, the Jefferson City Real Estate Association, and the Germania Club.

Murder-Suicide

Guests at the Bauer Hotel in June 1874 became victims of a shooting at the train station the next day. Zilie Auslin, a French immigrant, arrived in Jefferson City from St. Louis. She was in the company of Johannes Pierre, and they got a room claiming to be married. Auslin had left her husband, Leopold Hoelderle, a Prussian immigrant who operated a St. Louis saloon, which Pierre had frequented.

Auslin and Pierre planned to board the train the next day headed for Kansas City, but Hoelderle caught up with them. When Pierre saw Hoelderle coming, he ran from the train car and heard two pistol shots behind him, which missed. Hoelderle then entered the train car where Auslin sat, and she jumped from the train. However, she was struck by two fatal shots. Then Hoelderle turned the pistol on himself, firing twice more, which set his clothes on fire and ultimately took his life, as well.

New Pacific Hotel

James Willis Mabrey rented the hotel from Bauer beginning in 1876. It appears that this is when the name Pacific Hotel was adopted. The (second) Pacific Hotel emphasized boarding for travelers, and the A&P Dining Hall fed employees, travelers, and locals alike. Then, Henry Falk operated the hotel from about 1880 to 1883.

Whiskey Ring

Intrigue visited the hotel near the train station again in October 1875. Charles Jagau was brought to the hotel after being thrown from a train car window near the Round Grove Station. The St. Joseph man was on his way to testify before the federal court against his former employers involved in an alleged whiskey ring. Jagau regained his senses at the hotel long enough to recount how he had been taken by two men who chloroformed him before fatally pushing him off the train. The train backed up to retrieve the lost passenger, found to have been nearly strangled in a mud hole.

Building Boom

The Pacific Hotel was caught up in a local building boom in the early 1880s. Bauer made a significant addition to the Pacific Hotel in 1882 and then rebuilt altogether in 1884. Later, a light brick section was added to the west and then another addition south up Monroe Street.

At the same time, Bauer built a handsome, two-story brick home for himself at the corner of Lafayette and High Streets in 1883. Unfortunately, Bauer had only a few years to enjoy his new buildings. He was thrown from a "fiery, unbroken Texas pony" in August 1888, with severe injuries to his head, from which he died one month later.

Phil Schmidt

While the Bauer family maintained ownership, John Imhoff was proprietor of the new Pacific Hotel until 1887, when Phil Schmidt took charge. Schmidt emigrated from Westphalia, Prussia, to Jefferson City in 1858. After fighting for the Union in the Civil War, he conducted a popular saloon and boarding house at 219 East High Street for twenty-five years before taking on the railroad hotel.

When Schmidt married Mrs. Antonie Clara (Schneiderheize, widow Rattki) in September 1887, the couple was serenaded by the Little Six band at the Pacific Hotel that evening.

The Schmidt saloon could become a "perfect bedlam" when government laborers received their pay. For example, for three nights in 1892, the police kept two extra men on duty due to the revelry. "Many of the laborers will spend their last cent for intoxicants and then be left penniless and out of work," the *Tribune* said. About eighty of these men had been laid off until the river receded. Frequent fights, black eyes, and bloody noses resulted at Schmidt's place.

By 1896, William "Bill" Roetter, a grocery clerk, had the lease to the Pacific House. "[Bill] is a hustler and should make money out of his investment," the newspaper said.

Early Black Deputy

A Black deputy constable, Roscoe Berry, lost his firearm and badge after a misunderstanding in front of the Pacific Hotel in early 1916. Someone told police officer Lawrence Spurr that Berry was threatening to "get his scalp," so Spurr sought out Berry on the East End. The residents of the neighborhood had requested the appointment of a Black deputy constable and paid his per diem themselves.

After searching for a purse snatcher, Berry had gone from Lafayette Street to the depot. There, a Missouri Pacific detective harassed Berry, searched him, and found a .45 Colt revolver and tin star. When Berry said that he was an officer and resented the rough treatment, the detective said, "We will take care of you." After escorting him to the police station, the white officers learned that Berry had, in fact, been commissioned temporarily by Constable McKinley. Berry's commission was then revoked.

John Meyer

About 1900, John A. Meyer began more than thirty years' operation of the Pacific Hotel. In May 1905, he also bought the deed from the Bauer estate. Meyer had worked in eating houses for the Missouri Pacific after emigrating at age fifteen from Bavaria and was widely known among railroaders. Meyer added a new front door to the "old and well-known landmark," while making extensive improvements to the restaurant, combining it with the old lunchroom.

Meyer died in 1934, and his son Edgar Meyer continued operating the Pacific Hotel after serving three years in the U.S. Army during World War II, lasting until 1953.

Like many saloons in town, the Pacific had slot machines in 1936. When the police department decided to make citywide raids, they found two machines anchored with bricks at the Pacific. They were slowed removing these machines, giving time to notify other establishments to hide theirs. The January 1936 raid resulted in eighteen seizures from ten operators across town.

During World War II, troop trains stopping in Jefferson City would spill GIs into the depot and nearby saloons. The soldiers were seeking Anheuser

The (second) Pacific Hotel (*at left*) was opened in about 1855 at the southwest corner of Water and Monroe Streets. *Missouri State Archives.*

or Busch beer and had to be convinced that the local Capitol beer, by the Moerschel family's Capitol Brewing Company, was just as good, historian Walter Schroeder said. Three blocks up Monroe Street, the city's USO was next to the former county jail near the southeast corner with McCarty Street. But it only had cookies, coffee, and soft drinks.

Robert Burke

Robert J. Burke bought the hotel in April 1953. Previously, Burke had leased several local taverns, cocktail lounges, and cafés. The sprawling building had 69 feet on Water Street and 198 feet on Monroe Street. Burke found in the basement a collection of long-unused items, including soggy stacks of player piano rolls, brass bedsteads, green painted dressers, matchbooks from the Klondike, small arms cartridges in a box stamped "Bureau of Private Investigation," tear gas grenade boxes, chamber pots, and warranty deeds.

The Jefferson City Housing Authority used urban renewal laws to buy and raze the old Pacific Hotel in 1968. By then it had become a "dump" of liquor bottles, rotting mattresses, and broken furniture.

Second Missouri Hotel

1855–1941

With the railroad nearly completed in 1855, Charles B. Maus built a "new, large and commodious" brick hotel at the southeast corner of Water and Jefferson Streets, across the street from the Stone Warehouse, where he was in partnership with his brother-in-law, Charles Lohman.

Charles Maus opened the second Missouri Hotel in 1855. *Cole County Historical Society.*

Since the original hotel in the Crump building had changed its name to the Pacific Railroad Hotel, Maus adopted the name Missouri Hotel and leased operation to Bavarian baker Charles Feyerlein and William Andrea, a book binder. Of Feyerlein, the *Jefferson Inquirer* said that he was "a clever fellow [who] will make you at home." By

1856, Feyerlein was sole proprietor, and by the end of 1857, he had moved on to operating an oyster saloon at the corner of Washington and High Streets, dying two years later.

Veranda Hotel

In early 1856, the Veranda Hotel was built next door to the east of this (second) Missouri Hotel by city leader Jason Harrison. Inside, a reading room with current national journals was attached to the saloon.

Maryland-born Charles Eckler leased the new building. In 1854, Eckler had been a clerk on the *Steamship Timour* when it exploded three miles south of Jefferson City on the Missouri River. Eckler and his wife, Catherine (Fagin), with their four children, were aboard; three of the children were badly scalded.

Then Eckler operated the Veranda Saloon on High Street near the intersection with Madison, bringing the name Veranda with him to the hotel. Just one year after it opened, the Veranda Hotel burned, although most of the furniture was saved. Unexpectedly, Eckler died just two weeks later.

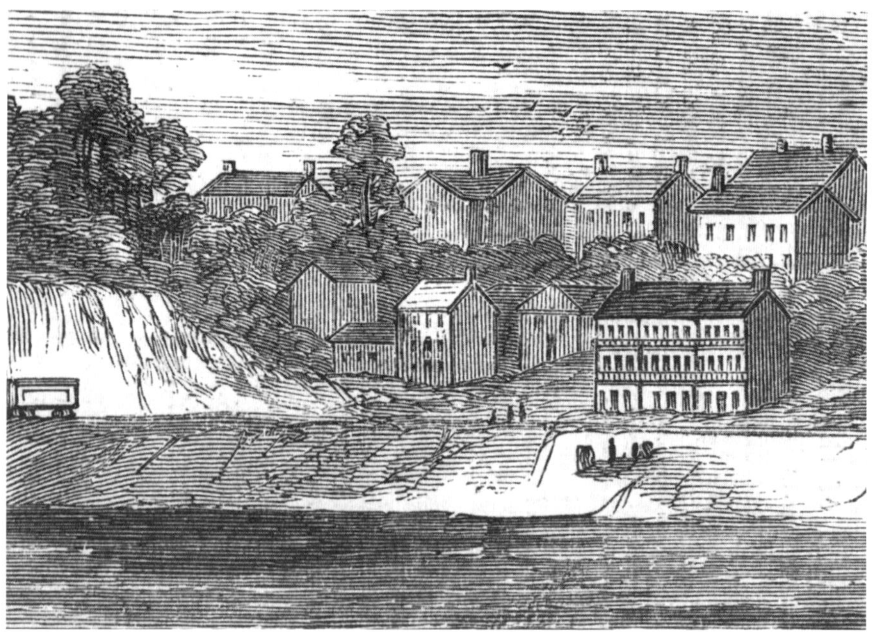

The Veranda Hotel is seen in this woodcut by Orlando Richardson that appeared in *Harper's Weekly* on July 6, 1861. *Missouri Historical Society.*

Widow Catherine Eckler then managed Maus' hotel, renaming the (second) Missouri Hotel as the Veranda Hotel. "Mrs. E. deserves the patronage of the public, for her energy in keeping a good house, and her perseverance in supporting a large family who depend entirely upon her industry for support," the *Jefferson City Inquirer* said.

By 1859, Maus was focused on his own mercantile. His wife had died, and so he had dissolved his partnership with his brother-in-law. On the lower floor of the Veranda Hotel was the wharf master's office, Maus' grocery, and steamboat agents' offices. The seven large double doors were convenient to freight traffic.

Union Hotel

Maus and his family fled Hesse-Darmstadt in 1829, but his father died in Pennsylvania and his mother in Ohio. Charles, being the youngest, moved with his sister and her husband to Jefferson City. He trained as a carpenter and stonemason before serving in the Mexican-American War.

When the Civil War came, Maus and some of his brothers joined the Union army, while other brothers served in the Confederacy. Returning from three years' service as captain of Company E of the Fifth Missouri State Militia Cavalry, Maus renamed his property the Union Hotel in honor of the victory.

Within a few years, the landing location was no longer optimal. Maus closed the hotel and moved his dry goods business in 1873 to the northeast corner of Jefferson and High Streets. The hotel property then became tenements and warehouses. This area around the north end of Jefferson Street later was dubbed Seventh Street, a derogatory reference to the street of ill-repute in St. Louis.

Second Jefferson House

George Washington Fifer Sr. came from Sedalia to manage a restaurant at 102 Jefferson Street, catering to railroad workers and known for excellent meals. Several of his sons worked for the Missouri Pacific, so in November 1904, Fifer leased the old Union Hotel building from Ernst Simonsen.

Simonsen bought the property from Louis Lohman, who had previously conducted a hotel in the building. Born in Sweden, Simonsen studied engineering in several countries. In 1888, he came to Jefferson City, buying

This 1940 photo by John Vachon shows the (second) Jefferson House, formerly the Union Hotel. *Library of Congress Farm Security Administration.*

the Bodine Lohman Agricultural Manufactory at the north end of Jefferson Street. This building he sold to the Bockrath Shoe Company. Simonsen also owned the Stone Warehouse (known today as Lohman's Landing), which he sold to the Tweedie Footwear Corporation.

George Fifer Jr. opened the (second) Jefferson House and Restaurant in the summer of 1905 at 110 Water Street. It was the second hotel location to use the name Jefferson. George Sr. sold his half-interest in the hotel to his son at the beginning of 1913. Fifer Jr. sold in 1925, when he was manager of the Jefferson City Produce Company.

Freda Hoffmeyer sold her home in Taos to take over the (second) Jefferson Hotel in Jefferson City, where she was assisted by her children. Charles H. Lister was proprietor by December 1935. After 1941, the building became the offices for the Tweedie Footwear Corporation.

Listed in the National Register of Historic Places in 1969, the former hotel was renovated as the state's official project for the nation's bicentennial in 1976. It is maintained by the Missouri Department of Natural Resources.

TENNESSEE HOUSE

1857–1899

The Tennessee House was the answer to some of the fretting of the local community and the complaints of the elected dignitaries over a lack of accommodations in the new era of railroads. The Capital City was in such a state that potential residents were being turned away because no housing was available for the full-time folks too.

Named for his native state, entrepreneur Dr. Tennessee Mathews built a forty-seven-room hotel at 114 East High Street in 1857. An observer called the Tennessee House "an ornament to our city." It had a seventy-foot-long dining room and a sixty-foot-long reception hall. The building was fifty-four by sixty feet, with an L-shaped annex running back ninety-two feet. The barroom was sixty by fourteen feet, and there was a parlor for the ladies.

Mathews partnered with Dr. A.W. Webb to roll out the endeavor. Webb was in charge of the dining room, bar, and office. North Carolinian Reuben Lee Bowden was the bartender but soon left to own his own grocery store. Sober, honest, and faithful, Bowden later served the city as overseer of the workhouse and as deputy marshal. Mr. Tryble was cook, assisted by Mr. Rienhat. "Tryble stands as high as any cook in the west, as we hear daily praise and commendation of the fare," the *Inquirer* said.

Next door, Mathews built in the same year a new brick drugstore, where he moved his City Drug Store and medical practice.

A.J. Irish brought his prior hotel experience and took over operation of the Tennessee House in July 1858. An expansion and general improvements were made in June 1859. McDaniel Dorriss, the first distiller in Jefferson City, served his own brew and operated the bar in the Tennessee House, while hotel management was turned over to Mathews' son, journalist Tennessee Mathews Jr.

In March 1863, Mathews added a large brick addition to accommodate an additional one hundred guests. C.P. Anderson, editor of the *Weekly California News* at the time, said that he "knows how to keep a hotel and the numerous guests, members of the legislature and others seemed to feel perfectly at home."

When Mathews added new furniture in about December 1865, the newspaper said that the Tennessee House "has no superior outside of St Louis in the state," with its large, airy rooms and its sense of home. "The doctor himself is one of nature's noblemen, true type of an old-time

The Tennessee House was opened in 1857 on the south side of High Street between Jefferson and Madison. *Missouri State Archives.*

gentleman, companionable and pleasant in his intercourse, sympathetic in his nature and courteous and polite to everyone," the *California Democrat* reported in February 1874.

By 1877, the only business left that had operated continually longer than Mathews' City Drug Store was the Obermayer Brothers Dry Goods Store.

Famous Correspondents

War correspondent William Fayel and famous explorer Henry Stanley met in the capitol rotunda in early 1867. Fayel was staying at the Tennessee House as the *St. Louis Republican* correspondent, and Stanley was stopping to give a lecture of his travels and misfortunes in Turkey at the city Market House.

Fayel then accompanied Stanley, a correspondent for the *New York Herald*, later that year on the Indian expedition under General Winfield Hancock. Four years later, Stanley would rescue Scottish missionary David Livingstone in the Congo. Fayel later served as a correspondent for the *New York Herald* in Turkey. Then he was secretary to U.S. Indian Commissioner Robert Campbell as he met with Native Americans throughout the West.

Tennessee Mathews

James Ford said in *A History of Jefferson City* that Tennessee Mathews dressed in a "Pickwickian style, swallowtail coat with large brass buttons, high collar and large bow tie."

Mathews' grandfather had served with General George Washington during the Revolutionary War and his father with General Andrew Jackson in the War of 1812.

As a teenager in Tennessee, Mathews worked cotton fields to pay for his primary education at Rock Spring Seminary. Mathews then taught school to pay for his law studies, being admitted to the Tennessee bar in 1831. That occupation paid for his courses at Louisville Medical College, from which he graduated in 1841.

Mathews practiced medicine for three years in Randolph County before settling in Jefferson City. He had several business partnerships through his medical practice and drugstore in his thirty-two years in Jefferson City. Several of these were students from the state university, such as Wilson Nicholas Melton, who later served with Confederate General Robert Lee. Another short-term partner was William Bettner, a Prussian who immigrated in 1825 after earning a medal for treating the wounds of Napoleon Bonaparte and who later practiced in Osage County.

When one of several seasons of cholera arrived in 1849, Mathews submitted a lengthy explanation of the disease and its spread to the *Weekly Jefferson Inquirer*, which filled several columns, ending, "Its great promoters are intemperance, privation and terror."

Beyond his own profession and enterprise, he was a community leader, from alderman and mayor to prison doctor, county coroner, and president of the fire department. He was a "pioneer of the cause of Temperance, as well as the faithful friend of all moral and charitable organizations," the *Tribune* said. Mathews also was active in the Cole County Agriculture and Mechanical Association.

The newspaper praised Mathews as "always foremost in the cause of improvement in our city." He was said to shy away from attention to his charity and kindness but was a man of decision, determination, and firm action.

Tennessee Mathews operated a drugstore and practiced medicine for decades in Jefferson City, as well as built the Tennessee House. *Cole County Historical Society.*

Before the Civil War, Mathews was a loyal Unionist who believed in the legality of slavery. In August 1860, he was president of the local Union Club, which had more than one hundred members. In March 1860, he aligned with a group that was for preservation of the Union at all hazards while "opposed to usurpation and tyrannical exercise of absolute and unlimited power of the chief, for supremacy of the constitution and opposed to secession," the *Glasgow Weekly Times* reported.

During the war, he was appointed magistrate to enforce civilian laws, particularly theft. That often made him a courtroom adversary of the Federal troops, but his decisions were sustained by higher courts. He personally dispensed nearly $2,000 in charity during that time, including for bonds to release citizens from the provost marshal and for preservation of the peace. He also filed a claim with the Union army for $1,200 damage to his garden, which supplied the hotel restaurant.

After the war, Mathews shifted his attention to his City Drug Store, already twenty years old, and converted from his Baptist upbringing to Catholicism. These changes were influenced by the sickness and death he saw among the soldiers he treated and from a significant carriage accident.

As justice of the peace, the *Tribune* said he was "a fearless, conscientious, faithful and intelligent magistrate." When the Jefferson City Fire Department reorganized in 1877, Mathews was elected president.

During an 1881 fire and riot at the Missouri State Penitentiary, Mathews took control of the situation. The warden opposed bloodshed, but the city believed that the inmates soon would be looting their homes and businesses. The militia was called in but waited outside the closed prison gates. Mathews grabbed a weapon and moved to the head of the mob, demanding the gates be opened. He moved so quickly into the prison yard that the inmates surrendered.

Of his hospitality, known statewide, it was said, "You are made to feel at home the moment you cross the threshold....Doctor himself is one of nature's noblemen, true type of an old-time gentleman, companionable and pleasant in his intercourse, sympathetic in his nature and courteous and polite to everyone," as a writer named Sorrell told the *California Democrat* in 1874.

Emma Colgan Sanford Mathews

Late in life, Mathews took his third wife, Emma (Colgan, widow Sanford). In 1845, Emma married War of 1812 veteran Alfred Sanford, who was thirty-eight years her senior. Mr. Sanford served one term as mayor before he died in 1863, leaving Emma a forty-three-year-old widow.

Emma's parents were Robert and Maria (Rogers) Colgan, who moved to Cote sans Dessein in about 1817 from Cape Girardeau, being in the furs and pelts trade. Her father came from Kentucky, but her mother was born in Missouri to French parents. Emma remembered helping load guns for her father in defense of their home on the Gasconade River when they were attacked by Native Americans.

Mrs. Sanford entered the hospitality business at the Capitol House at 101 Washington Street, with "particular attention to accommodate members of the General Assembly [since it] is much nearer the Capitol building than any other boarding house in the city," the *Missouri State Times* said.

After the war, she took over the American House, opposite the Pacific Railroad depot. Four years later, she opened the "Ladies and Gents' Restaurant and Day Board" on High Street, near Riddler's Drug Store. After being arrested and fined $50 (about $1,400 in 2025 dollars) by Marshal John Cohagan for keeping a bawdy house, Mrs. Sanford returned to the Capitol House.

In September 1875, Mrs. Sanford leased the Tennessee House, just after its large expansion. "Well and favorably known" Sanford was considered "worthy and deserving" for her experience and knowledge as a hotel hostess.

She was also longtime matron of the Missouri State Penitentiary. The newspaper said that she provided "motherly care to her most unfortunate charge" and that she was an "almost indispensable auxiliary." Her state report in 1882 said that discipline was the key to preventing brooding and inspiring cheerfulness.

Matthews and Sanford were married December 18, 1884, at the Tennessee House. A large number of friends attending and brought many valuable gifts. He was seventy-seven to her sixty-five. But they had three years together.

Metropolitan Hotel

When Mathews died in 1887, the name of the Tennessee Hotel was changed to the Metropolitan Hotel, and management was transferred to Enos C. Barton, a native of Cole County. A courteous gentleman, Barton spent only six months here before returning to the (second) Indiana House, at the corner of Washington and Stewart Streets.

The Jefferson City public school began renting rooms in the old hotel in 1886, as it was in need of a new building but hadn't passed a bond to build yet. However, it clearly was not adapted for school use with low ceilings and no playground. The parlor and dining rooms served as classrooms. A business school was opened inside in February 1889, taught by Cora Titsworth.

Despite modernizing the front in 1890, the old Tennessee House was demolished in June 1899 by Schwartz and Brown. George Porth, a jeweler who moved to Jefferson City in 1879, bought the lots. The present-day three-story, red brick building at 110–114 East High Street was built by John Vogt, J.H. Edwards, and George Porth. Originally Porth Jewelry, it later housed Meyerhardt's Men's Wear.

RANSOM-CAPITOL HOUSE

1858–1906

William H. Kolkmeyer built a forty-room, four-story brick rooming house for George B. Ransom in November 1858 at 101 Washington Street, next door to the capitol grounds. The site had been the livery stable of Thomas Kelly, as well as the blacksmith shop of William Brocksmith.

Born in Virginia, Ransom was a farmer in Callaway County and owned considerable land and enslaved people. Ransom held several political seats,

The Ransom House (*center of image*) was the closest hotel to the Capitol building at the north end of Washington Street. *Library of Congress.*

including county surveyor and coroner, and was a teacher and a charter member of the local masons Carter Lodge.

During the war, the Ransom House was used as the Union hospital. After the war, Ransom rented the boarding house to a man named Rice, formerly a Confederate captain, who later became commissioner of the permanent seat of government.

Capitol House

Many legislative committees held their meetings in the front rooms of the Ransom House, due to minimal space in the capitol. "Doubtless many important bills were talked over there and possibly some boodle exchanged hands," the *Republican Review* said.

Ransom sold his Capitol House to Dr. Alexander "Sandy" McDonald Davison, who thoroughly remodeled and repaired it in late 1873 with thirty-three good-sized rooms, while also converting the dining room into a saloon. The *Daily State Journal* described it as the "snuggest and best apportioned" local hotel. Davison then left the operation to M.E. Eiker, L.W. Painter, and Emma (Colgan) Sanford, who later managed the Tennessee House.

Daniel Wade from Elston bought the hotel at a mortgage sale in 1878 with adjoining houses on Stewart Street, a site briefly considered for the location of the Old Supreme Court building.

Second Indiana House

Later adopting the name of the (second) Indiana House in 1884, William A. Lockwood made it a "quiet and genteel place," said the *State Times*. By 1886, Lockwood had retired to farm living "preferring the pleasures and freedom of farm life," the *State Times* noted. When Herman Schulte bought the four-story building from the Wade estate in 1906, he replaced it with two flats. Today, the lot is part of the capitol's south lawn.

Part V

1861 to 1865

Leading up to the Civil War, nearly all of the hotel operators were of southern roots. Yet most continued during the war.

After the Union army arrived in June 1861, it was an occupying force throughout the rest of the war. Hotels were commandeered as hospitals, fortifications, and barracks. Others were filled with officers and refugees fleeing guerrillas in the county. By far, there was more demand than availability for sleeping rooms.

Keeping a boarding house was a steady revenue stream for many widows and single women. It was also an imperative in the early Capital City, when every two years the small town was flooded with special visitors, dignitaries, and urgent guests.

In 1860, the following residents kept boarding houses or rooms above their saloons: Bernard and Henrietta Bruns, Levi Gunsaullus, William and Georgetta Buffington, Elizabeth Gunn, John and Mary Hanigan, Israel and Mary Read, Fred Knaup, Margaret Feinlein, John and Magdalena Schott, Emily Chiles, Susan and Elizabeth Basye, Mary Lusk, Caroline Groll, Catharine Eckles, and Emily Lansdown.

These were in addition to the hotels operating at the start of the Civil War: City Hotel by Hardin and Margaret Newman, Tennessee House by Tennessee Mathews, McCarty House by Burr and Alzira McCarty, the Ransom House by George Ransom, Virginia Hotel by William and Henrietta Kerr, Ferguson House by William and Sarilda Ferguson, and the Jefferson House by John and Patsy Curry.

Even the short-lived Capital Hotel kept a good business during the war. John and Mary Hanigan, Irish and French immigrants, respectively, built the three-story brick house on Madison Street across from the Governor's Mansion in 1858. Near the corner of Main Street, it was conveniently next door to the U.S. Post Office, where stagecoaches stopped daily. The *State Times* was "agreeably surprised at the comfort and taste" of the furniture, carpeting, and modern improvements. However, they lost the property in an 1860 sheriff's sale. It appears that Thomas and Margaret Mills took over but that the property continued to change hands frequently.

Bruns Boarding House

1853–1877

Perhaps the most well-remembered of these boarding houses was one operated by Dr. Bernard and Jette Bruns, although it was not long in use.

Born in Stromberg, Westphalia, Henrietta "Jette" (Geisberg) Bruns married Dr. Johann Bernhard Bruns in 1832 and followed him in 1835 to Missouri, where they helped to found the community of Westphalia. She is best known for her letters published in *Hold Dear as Always: A German Immigrant Life in Letters*.

The family moved to Jefferson City in 1853, opening their three-story boarding house at the southeast corner of High and Washington Streets. The next year, in 1854, Dr. Bruns built a mercantile at the northeast corner of High and Madison Streets, where he continued his medical practice.

Their boarders primarily had been elected officials and distinguished visitors who were friends of Dr. Bruns. He was described as a "man of irreproachable character," by the *Inquirer* when he served as city alderman.

From their boarding house, Mrs. Bruns and her husband watched the rebel loyalists gather on the capitol lawn with Confederate General Sterling Price before fleeing west with Governor Claiborne Jackson in June 1861. In the first days of Union occupation that followed, the wounded and sick soldiers were brought to the Bruns Boarding House for care.

One of the saddest events of the war occurred outside the Brunses' front door. On a Saturday evening in September 1863, seven-year-olds Fannie Dale and Albertina Bergau were playing on the corner of Washington and High Streets near the Gunsaullus boarding house. Across High Street, a

The Bruns Boarding House was opened at the southeast corner of Washington and High Streets, as seen in this 1859 lithograph by Eduard Robyn. *Brooks Collection.*

Union soldier was sitting on the Brunses' steps when his weapon discharged, passing through both girls' stomachs. Both were daughters of Union officers, the latter of a local druggist.

The war took a toll on Dr. Bruns, who was elected the city's first German-speaking mayor in 1862. Their son Henry was the first soldier from Cole County known to be killed in action, falling at the Battle of Iuka on July 7, 1863. Then Dr. Bruns died in the spring of 1864, leaving Jette to manage their property and debts while rearing four children and two of her brother's children.

That also left Jette Bruns to operate the boarding house, which thrived during the legislative session with friends of the doctor. She would not take in Democrats or former secessionists. But former slaveholder and German-speaking immigrant Arnold Krekel, then a federal judge, often came to dinner in her home, which he called "the radical corner." Jette Bruns sold the three-story brick boarding house in 1877.

LANSDOWN BOARDING HOUSE

1855–1902

The Lansdown Boarding House at 418 Madison Street, was operated by three unmarried sisters from Virginia. They brought with them their southern manners and hospitality, but also their dependence on enslaved people.

Emily, Lizzie, and Nancy expanded their home as a means of income after the death of their older brother, George, in 1855. "Under Miss Emily's effective management, the business was financially successful," according to William Henry Lansdown descendants. At one point, the sisters even leased nearby dwellings to accommodate all of their guests.

Their boarders were professionals, tradesmen and laborers, as well as the biennial politicians. They also cared for their invalid brother, Edwin, and a few elderly widows.

While the Lansdown Boarding House brought the sisters an income, the daily work was carried out by enslaved Caroline. She went to bed after midnight and was up before dawn, sleeping on a pallet on the floor of a closet off the kitchen.

Caroline milked the cows, churned the butter, prepared three regular meals and served individual meals, washed the dishes, swept and scrubbed the floors, did daily dusting, washed windows, made up the beds, did the laundry, emptied and cleaned chamber pots, carried the water up and down the stairs for guest's baths, and fed kindling into individual room fireplaces. Caroline also nursed elderly and sick boarders, even through yellow fever and smallpox. Despite all that, if she was seen sitting down, she was chided as lazy and could be beaten for offenses as minor as serving cold coffee.

While Caroline was enslaved at the Lansdown Boarding House, her cooking was popular. Guests not staying at the house would wait in line for a seat at the dining table. After emancipation, the Lansdown sisters dismissed her. Taking the name Caroline Edwards, she became a sought-after cook by local hotel restaurants, including the City Hotel, and hosted a popular stand at community events and county fairs.

The Lansdown sisters continued their boarding house, though of lesser reputation, after the war, even adding rooms in 1871. The sisters adopted Caroline's son, William Henry, who took their surname rather than his father's, Jack Lacy, and paid for his education at Lincoln Institute. He became a distinguished educator in Texas until the sisters asked him to return and take care of them in their old age.

This he did, and his wife, Sarah (Young), kept the house. Emily's will left all their property, after the deaths of Nancy and Lizzie, to William as their sole heir.

However, when the last sister died in 1903, William and his wife were kicked out of the house. Half nieces and nephews in Virginia, who the sisters had never met, were sought to contest the will as Lansdown heirs. When William and Sarah filed suit just for their services in caring for the elderly women, the court denied all of his $1,625 claim and allowed only $156 of her $455 claim. Having been pushed out of the local school as well, William Henry Lansdown became a caller and custodian for the Missouri Pacific Railroad for the next twenty-seven years until his death.

Lusk-Nichols House

1844–1913

The original home of Pennsylvanians William and Mary (Fitzsimmons) Lusk may be the longest-lasting boarding house in Jefferson City. The wife and mother of local newspapermen, Mary Lusk opened her home to legislators, judges, and other dignitaries while they operated the *Jefferson Inquirer*. For example, in 1844, thirteen legislators were rooming at the Lusk Home, on the north side of the 100 block of West High Street.

The Lusks moved to Missouri in the mid-1830s and built their home before 1840 with a view of the state capitol. William Lusk Sr. died in 1844, leaving

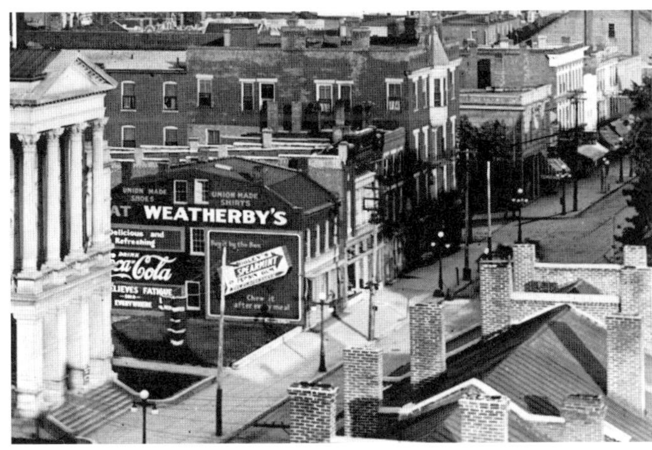

The Lusk Home, which became the Nichols House, was located just west of the Central Hotel until 1913. *Missouri State Archives.*

Mary Lusk to rear their children still at home and to help their eldest son, James Lusk, to operate the newspaper. When James Lusk died in 1858, the second son William H. Lusk Jr. took over the newspaper. When the younger William's wife died in 1859, Mary Lusk also reared her granddaughter, Mary Bell Lusk.

To provide additional income, Mary Lusk built a second boarding house next door to the east at 108 West High Street, between her home and the Virginia Hotel. Her daughter, Mary Ann Lusk, continued operating the boarding house until Mary Bell married. The original family home was replaced in 1882 with a brick commercial building.

Newlyweds Joseph and Regina (Braun) Huegel took charge of the six-room boarding house in 1872. Two years later, they moved next door to manage the Virginia Hotel.

Nichols House

Samuel Nichols left management of the Jefferson House in 1874 to buy the Lusk House, which he renamed the Nichols House. Although Samuel Nichols and his wife, Elizabeth (Moore), only kept the house for a few years, the name stuck for decades. The *Tribune* called Nichols "one of the most gallant gentlemen at the Capital."

By far, the most notable event related to this boarding house was its involvement in the U.S. Supreme Court decision to reverse the Civil Rights Act of 1875. Nichols was arrested in the fall of 1876, after W.H.R. Agee, an African American delegate from Daviess County to the Republican convention in Jefferson City, was denied accommodation at the Nichols House.

The case against Nichols was combined with four cases from other states to be heard by the U.S. Supreme Court in 1883. The Stanley case from Kansas also was related to hotel accommodations. The Ryan and Singleton cases from California and New York involved theaters, and a Tennessee case involving Robinson and wife addressed railcar seating. The Supreme Court's eight-to-one decision said that the Fourteenth Amendment did not allow Congress to tell private individuals what to do in their business.

Born in Kentucky, Samuel Nichols was a child when his family moved to Boone County. He kept a farm in Callaway County and later Boone County. After four years at the Nichols House, his family operated a hotel in Colorado one year. Then they returned because "Uncle Sam thinks there is no place like Missouri after all," the *Jefferson City Tribune* said. Nichols then kept a hotel in Ashland.

Caroline (Luck) Hollingsworth and her daughters kept the Nichols House, 112 West High Street, for about five years until 1883. Hollingsworth was born in Virginia and married a miller in Marion County. After his death, they came to Jefferson City and later operated a boarding house in St. Louis.

In 1883, William A. Lockwood leased the Nichols House, which sat on the lot adjacent to the site selected for the new U.S. Courthouse and Post Office. One year later, Lockwood took charge of the (second) Indiana House, and Mrs. L. Conn became proprietress of the Nichols House. She passed it to Henry Schwartzott.

Louise Gray

Mrs. Louise (Hunter) Gray began twenty-five years at the Nichols House in May 1886. She was born and reared near Russellville, and her hospitality was known for its "good meals, comfortable beds, [and] airy rooms," the *Illustrated Sketchbook* said. Mrs. Gray came to Jefferson City in 1877 from Arrow Springs. Her obituary remembered the fifty-nine-year-old as a "true Christian [and] good woman."

In the late 1890s, while Mrs. Gray operated the Nichols House, her sister Mrs. Jennie (Hunter) Scott was in charge of the Scott House on Monroe Street, just south of the railroad depot. The sisters were proud of their housekeeping, learned from their mother, who emigrated from Scotland.

After Mrs. Gray's death in 1912, Joseph Huegel at the Central Hotel bought the Nichols House, razing it 1913.

Part VI

1866 to 1879

The years following the Civil War showed a shift in societal norms, such as more German-speaking residents operating the more prestigious hotels, including Fred Knaup at the City Hotel and Joseph Huegel at the Virginia Hotel. Formerly enslaved men also found advantageous positions as cooks and porters at these hotels, including U.S. Colored Troops veteran Richard Winston, who was porter at the City Hotel, and Henry Barnes, who was a noted cook at the City Hotel and then the Hotel Madison. Others of southern leanings chose to leave, like Hardin Newman, who left the City Hotel to operate a hotel in St. Louis.

Jefferson City fared well in the years following the Civil War. In fact, several years showed booming construction, each exceeding the last. In 1871, that included the present Governor's Mansion, a new county jail, the Methodist church, Harmonia Hall, George Wagner's Beer House, Elizabeth Gunn's brick row houses on Madison Street, the prison deputy warden's house, and Oscar Burch's house on Jefferson Street.

The next year, construction included Judge W.C. Young's home on Capitol, Henry Bragg's business block (later to become the old city hall), B. Gratz Brown's row on Capitol, and the stone lodge and walls at the Jefferson City National Cemetery.

Sedalia was still vying for the capital to be relocated. In that effort, it received the Missouri Pacific Railroad Company's machine shops, despite Jefferson City already clearing ground for the same promise. "We have endeavored to arouse our people of Jefferson to a thorough comprehension of the labor that lies before them and which must be accomplished before the city can be assured that its future is no longer precarious and contingent. It is not enough that we have the Capital of a great state. Of this distinction we are liable at any time to be robbed," the newspaper said.

Assessed valuations in 1873 reveal hotel operators to be among the city's wealthiest property holders. Nearly doubling the second-highest valuation, General Thomas Lawson Price's estate topped the list at $120,000 (about $3.1 million in 2025 dollars). Fifth and sixth were George Wagner and Fred Knaup, followed by Burr McCarty and Tennessee Mathews.

The city had fifteen grocery stores, eleven saloons, eight hotels, seven dry good stores, five bakeries and five millineries, four barbers and four drugstores, three billiard saloons, two lumber stores, and more. Among professionals, there were eleven lawyers, six physicians, three blacksmiths, two dentists, two photographers, two tailors, two jewelers, and a watchmaker. Manufacturing also was thriving with five shoemakers, four furniture makers, three cigar makers, two saddle makers, one marble works, a soda manufacturer, a brewery, a book-bindery, and a farm machinery manufacturer.

John Ray, editor of the *Cassville Democrat*, reported in 1875:

> *Jefferson City is a peculiar looking city of some 5,000 inhabitants—built in long straggling streets, on hills, and hill sides, with many intervening gullies and ravines.*
>
> *But the many fine public buildings, and private residences, gives it quite a picturesque appearance. Its inhabitants are rather cosmopolitan in their character; but at the same time extremely courteous and agreeable.*
>
> *What strikes a stranger most forcibly, when he first arrives at this city, is the number of dram shops and boarding houses, which are to be seen on every hand. Creature comforts are therefore plentiful; but they are costly for good boarding cannot be obtained for less than $7 per week, while at some of the hotels it is as high as $12.*

In 1876, the population jumped to seven thousand residents, and the city boasted eight churches, a female college, a public high school, three banks, Dulle's flour mill, Wallendorf's sawmill, a carding factory, Wagner's brewery, an agricultural implement factory, and three furniture shops. Mrs. Ella Matson was the postmistress.

Extra Business

In addition to the hotel business itself, the larger hotels provided sample rooms for traveling salesmen to set up their wares or services. Medical specialists, like dental surgeons and eye doctors, would see patients for a few weeks. New technology, like sewing machines or washing machines, would be on display in sample rooms. In 1899, Christ Miller boasted that the City Hotel had the largest sample rooms in the state.

The first floor of the larger hotels often housed storefronts, rented from the hotel. Nearly every site had a saloon and a barber. In the early days, the lucky ones housed the stagecoach offices or the telegraph stations.

Dr. Tennessee Mathews kept his own drugstore under his Tennessee House, and the local *Tribune* rented space. At the City Hotel, shops included tobacco, watch and jewelry, clothing, shoes and books.

Several established businesses began as start-ups underneath a local hotel, like J.T. Craven's Grocery or Abe Heim's Clothing.

In the early twentieth century, outdoor theaters called airdomes were constructed behind the Madison House and the Monroe House. Although a short-lived phenomenon, the theaters attracted quality traveling shows, as well as providing the earliest form of moving pictures. The Madison House Airdome seated 1,600 and was filled to capacity nearly every night in its first season.

Despite the emphasis on retaining the capital and the growth in industry and construction, hoteliers still struggled with maintaining St. Louis–quality hotels, as they filled to capacity for only a few months every two years. City Hotel owner Fred Knaup once wished that Jefferson City hotels could be made of India rubber, so they could be inflated or collapsed as an occasion required, based on the transient business.

New City Hotel

circa 1836–1916

One of the iconic hotels of Jefferson City's past was the City Hotel at the northwest corner of High and Madison Streets. A new post–Civil War era

Fred Knaup bought the City Hotel at the northwest corner of Madison and High Streets in 1867. *Cole County Historical Society.*

began in May 1867 at the hands of Fred Knaup. The Prussian-born carriage maker had operated a saloon, grocery, and boarding house on Main Street "nearly opposite the Missouri Pacific Railroad Depot," called the (third) Missouri Hotel, during the war.

Immediately after purchasing the iconic building from the Newman family, Knaup added a third story to the twenty-seven-year-old brick hotel. His expansion included space on the main floor for large business rooms, including tailor Solomon Leopold and the *State Journal* newspaper.

In 1874, the landings to the High Street entrance were lengthened and the office moved from the second floor to the main floor. The remodel "spared neither labor pains nor expense to suitably arrange the building and most gorgeously furnish it," the *State Journal* noted.

Knaup bought the building north of the hotel, owned by Christ Wagner and occupied by the Barnes and Lane restaurant, in 1878. A third story was added, allowing him to rearrange the hotel layout and add "eight commodious rooms." Each room featured a walnut furniture suite by the local company Stampfli and Karges, plus marble-top tables and stands. The first-floor saloon was connected to a large club room, and the office was returned to the second floor.

The general manager was Henry Klette, described as pleasant, agreeable, and attentive, with an extensive acquaintance with commercial tourists and the traveling public. An English immigrant, Klette was a corporal for three years in Company H of the Fourth New York Cavalry. He lived in the Knaup home for forty-four years, as clerk and servant, until his death in 1910 at the St. James Union Soldiers Home.

Howard Barnes

The dining room was moved to the basement, where "all modern conveniences will be found…under the superintendence of Howard Barnes assisted by John Lane, two of the most popular caterers in the state," according to the *People's Tribune* in 1878. Howard Barnes came to Jefferson City before the war and was the first Black restaurant operator in the city. He bought his freedom after being camp cook in the 1849 gold rush to California from Howard County with the Boggs family, who enslaved him.

Howard Barnes cooked in hotel kitchens, was a caterer and cook for camping trips, and operated his own restaurant, the Delmonico. His restaurant "was the resort of all the prominent public men who visited the capital during and between sessions of legislature. He knew them all and can relate interesting anecdotes of peculiarities and characteristics of some of Missouri's early-day statesmen and politicians.…Many have been the political conferences and the making and breaking of political slates over the venison steaks and other culinary delicacies with which Uncle Howard tempted his patrons," reported the *State Republican*.

Even Eugene Field, briefly a government correspondent and a children's author, was fond of Barnes' cooking, writing to a Chicago newspaper from Europe that "he would give $50 if he could be back in Uncle Howard's restaurant for one single meal of roast 'coon," said the *Daily Tribune*.

Becoming comparatively wealthy, Barnes was able to help Lincoln Institute fund its first building. Also active in Republican politics, he was proposed as possibly the first Black candidate for mayor and for school board. In 1880, he was the "the first and only colored man who has ever been on the state ticket," as a candidate for railroad commissioner, according to the *State Journal*.

Fred Knaup

Fred Knaup arrived in Jefferson City in about 1853 and served multiple terms as an alderman and twenty-five years on the school board. He was on the board of directors of First National Bank and was involved in the ill-fated Standard Shoe Company.

His Italian-style home at the southeast corner of Adams and Main Streets brought the first indoor plumbing to the city. The attic had a tank filled with forced water from the cistern. The brick and stone home designed and built by Fred Binder was the "costliest and best appointed" house built in 1877, the *State Times* said.

Knaup was the third-highest taxpayer in Cole County in 1880, after National Bank and Mrs. Carrie V. Price, even above the Exchange Bank, brewer George Wagner, banker Joseph Clark, and miller G.H. Dulle. In 1886, he was the sixth wealthiest, having been surpassed by Wagner and Clark, as well as saloon keeper John G. Schott and merchant Frank Rephlo.

Fred Knaup immigrated as a wagonmaker and retired from hotelkeeping as one of the wealthiest men in Jefferson City. *Ruthie Caplinger.*

Knaup was praised as a "man of great energy and industry...of foresight and conservative business habits...one of the most enterprising, public-spirited men in the city." The *People's Tribune* of 1878 concluded, "If every citizen would copy his example, we would have a better town very soon."

Among the early German-speaking arrivals, Knaup was an unofficial greeter and sponsor. He helped many get their start in the area, like Joseph Zeisberg. In his memoirs, Zeisberg said that he was picked up in 1881 at the old railroad depot by porter Richard Winston, a former U.S. Colored Troops soldier, and taken wherever he needed to go. Zeisberg said that Knaup treated him to "bountiful meals and comfortable bed" until he could connect with his relatives in the rural area, historian Walter Schroeder said.

Mary Knaup was a progressive woman for her day, graduating from college, working in her father's hotel, and promoting the expansion of the local library. *Ruthie Caplinger.*

Mary Knaup

Knaup's daughter, Mary, by age seventeen, had taken charge of the household department "to make it pleasant for ladies who may seek rest or recreation in the new city." She was the firstborn of five children to Fred and Margret (Blochberger) Knaup. She was confirmed at the Evangelical Lutheran Church but active in the Presbyterian Church later in life. Mary Knaup was involved in the Germania Club and Harmonie Society as a young person. While helping her father's business, she also attended Christian College in Columbia.

Annually, Mary Knaup was involved in preparations for Decoration Day, as well as creating elaborate costumes for masked balls. She contributed her vocal music talents to many community events. She was described as a "sensible homebody." Mary Knaup was longtime vice-president of the Jefferson City Library Association, and her sister, Frieda, was assistant librarian.

John Kaiser

John Baptiste Kaiser began managing the City Hotel in 1871, and then after thirteen years at the City Hotel, he bought the neighboring Hotel Madison. Kaiser was held as a prisoner of war during the 1848 German Revolution. He escaped in 1849, fleeing first to Virginia before taking up construction in Glasgow. Before the war, Kaiser had been a hotelier in Boonville. In the Civil War, he served four years in the Boonville Battery Home Guards and then the Fifth Missouri State Militia Cavalry, reaching the rank of major. "He was an active and energetic officer and a terror to bushwhackers in this part of the state," the *Tribune* said.

Back to Knaup

When Kaiser left the City Hotel, Knaup expanded again to keep up with the modernizations at the Hotel Madison. In 1885, the third floor of the next adjoining building on Madison Street, known as the Scovern Building, featured a short-lived public roller-skating rink on the third floor. Knaup converted the second and third floors to guest rooms and allowed the grocery store to remain on the main floor. At this time, the main entrance was moved from High Street to Madison Street.

While the Hotel Madison sought politicians and the Monroe House railroad men, the City Hotel boasted the largest sample room in the state to appeal to traveling salesmen.

The City Hotel under Knaup made several expansions north on Madison Street. This is how it looked in 1891, when sketched by Frederick Suden. *Missouri State Archives.*

George Pope took over the City Hotel in 1890, when he gave it a "general fixing up," including "one of the finest water filters in the country."

Christ Miller

Ben Vieth and Christ Miller bought the City Hotel in January 1893 from Fred Knaup for $30,000 (about $1 million in 2025 dollars). Miller bought out Vieth's share three years later.

Miller was bartender at the Monroe House four years before he and Vieth bought the Cornell Brothers saloon at 226 Madison Street, renaming it the Vieth & Miller Saloon in 1890.

An avid outdoorsman, Miller participated in local gun clubs, as well as regular outings for hunting and fishing. His other community involvements during his nine years operating the City Hotel included serving as director of the Jefferson City Bridge Company in 1893, Third Ward alderman in 1895, and organizer of the Retail Liquor Dealers Association in 1897.

After selling his early 1902, Miller was an officer of both the Republican-styled newspaper and the Jefferson City Sand Company. When he lost the election for the city collector in November 1902, Miller bought the Senate

Bar at 129 East High Street from Alex Kluth. Miller again was elected Third Ward alderman in 1904, the same year he was made a charter member of the local Order of Eagles. By 1910, he had retired from the Miller-Enloe Buffet on Madison Street, selling to partner Lawrence Enloe.

Central Missouri Trust

By 1900, the City Hotel had forty-five, well-lit and ventilated individual rooms, a buffet room, and dining room. The Gordon & Church real estate firm, representing Central Missouri Trust Company, paid Miller $36,000 (about $1.3 million in 2025 dollars) in March 1902 for the corner lot. The site continued as office building, hotel, and saloon until 1916. It was razed and replaced with the present seven-story Carthage stone building, Jefferson City's "first skyscraper."

Hotel Madison

1869–1939

William Dangerfield Meredith moved from Virginia to Jefferson City in 1833 and built his house on the southwest corner of Madison and Main Streets. A carpenter on the second capitol construction, he was the city's first police constable and was in charge at the time of the first homicide not involving the Missouri State Penitentiary.

Later, this prominent corner became a book bindery. Situated across from the Governor's Mansion, only two blocks east of the capitol and two blocks southwest of the railroad depot, it was an ideal location.

Log and frame business houses filled the west side of Madison Street, from the *Examiner* office north to Main Street, in the late 1860s. After fire claimed all of them, Frank Schmidt bought the entire corner in 1869.

Schmidt House

"Old fogies doubted when he bought the corner to build a hotel," a 1900 news account said. In addition to transforming the corner, Schmidt's House featured three female office clerks—his wife and two stepdaughters.

After amassing his fortune in construction, Schmidt opened a retail store specializing in wallpaper, window glass, looking glass, and picture frames. This he sold to Francis Roer, investing everything in his hotel.

Schmidt's $60,000 (about $1.5 million in 2025 dollars) hotel was ambitious in 1869. The imposing structure was brick with eighty-five rooms and the most modern conveniences. Rooms were well aired and had attached balconies; some were even designed as family suites. It had a 60-foot-square billiard room and a 105-by-60-foot concert hall, the first in town.

Before construction was complete, Schmidt's rooms were nearly sold out.

Pulitzer Shootout

In January 1870, a famous shootout occurred in the Schmidt barroom. Young immigrant Joseph Pulitzer had been elected state representative from St. Louis, but he continued as correspondent for the *Westliche Post*.

One of Pulitzer's political hallmarks was eradicating corruption in St. Louis County. Pulitzer proposed legislation, which eventually passed, for reform. This drew out lobbyists in opposition. Captain Edward Augustine had been treated generously by the St. Louis County Court, with offices and contracts, so he took some of Pulitzer's views in the *Post* personally.

The Schmidt House, only two blocks east of the capitol, was already a gathering place for politicians. Many of the St. Louis crowd were in the parlor at about 7:00 p.m. on January 27, 1870, when Augustine approached Pulitzer with his finger pointed at the journalist's nose, accusing him of printing lies.

Pulitzer walked out of the barroom. He was rooming on High Street, a few blocks from the Schmidt House, perhaps at the Bruns Boarding House or Wagner Hotel, both operated by German-speakers at the time. From his room, Pulitzer retrieved his four-barreled Sharp's pistol.

Returning to the Schmidt House parlor, Pulitzer renewed the insulting argument. Augustine called Pulitzer a "puppy," and Pulitzer returned with the accusation of "liar." When Augustine, by far the larger man, made a menacing approach, Pulitzer fire twice. The lobbyist managed to deflect the shots, one hitting his knee and the other the floor.

"Schmidt's hotel had never seen such excitement," W.A. Swamberg said in the biography *Pulitzer*.

The next day, Pulitzer was fined $5 for breach of peace and arraigned for assault to kill. Twenty-one months later, he was fined $100 and court costs for the assault.

Fire

After just two years of admiration, flames were seen early one morning in March 1871 rising from the southeast corner of the Schmidt House roof. Thankfully, printers were already at work nearby at the *State Times* and rushed to rouse the slumbering guests. Only four or five of the eighty-five rooms were not occupied that night, yet all walked to safety.

Frank Schmidt and his wife, Kunigunda (Korn), had invested about $125,000 (just more than $3 million in 2025 value), but it was insured for only $46,000. The fire crippled his finances. The remnants of their fine brick hotel and the lot went up to a trustee's sale on April 14, 1871.

Schmidt, who had emigrated from Prussia, returned to construction to regain his fortune. His many bridges included the first railroad bridge across the Osage River, as well as "many large buildings that are a monument to his memory," included his own home at 526 East Capitol Avenue and the Dallmeyer Building at 206–210 East High Street, according to James Ford in *A History of Jefferson City*.

Grand Duke Alexis

Despite the financial setbacks of the fire, Schmidt continued his duties as city mayor. One of those was making a strong case for a public fire company. Another was to greet dignitaries visiting the city.

In January 1872, nine months after the devastating Schmidt House fire, Mayor Schmidt greeted Grand Duke Alexis when he stopped at Jefferson City during his buffalo hunt in the United States. The Grand Duke's rented train at $3,500 per day (about $90,000 per day in 2025 dollars) came from the west to the city's modest railroad platform.

Local crowds assembled at the depot before the 9:30 a.m. arrival, and the Siegel Battery set up on the capitol terrace. Seven local carriages collected the Russian contingent, which included frontiersman William "Buffalo Bill" Cody. This was not, however, Cody's first time in Jefferson

City. As a Union scout, Cody helped defend the city in the fall of 1864 against the threat of Confederate General Sterling Price's raid.

The procession visited the capitol, where the Grand Duke made a brief speech to the General Assembly, then they dined at the Executive Mansion with Governor B. Gratz Brown, state officers, Supreme Court judges, federal judge Arnold Krekel, journalist Joseph Pulitzer, and many others.

The Grand Duke received callers that afternoon in the first floor parlors of the newly rebuilt Hotel Madison, where Mayor Schmidt made the introductions. The foreign dignitary handed out presents to onlookers at the train station before he departed.

Dr. William Curry

The trustee for the Schmidt House, J.L. Smith, sold "all property not absolutely destroyed by the fire" to William A. Curry, whose parents operated the Jefferson House. However, Schmidt had salvaged doors, window sashes, and blinds from the remains. That led to lawsuits that reached the Missouri Supreme Court in February 1874, when the court decided Schmidt had a right to what he collected.

Curry rebuilt the hotel on the convenient corner in late 1871 with partner Oscar Burch and named it the Hotel Madison. When U.S. Senator Frank Blair visited in January 1872, citizens showed up to serenade him while he appeared on the hotel balcony.

After serving in the Mexican-American War, Curry attended the University of Virginia. During the 1850s, he was physician at the Missouri

The Hotel Madison was built in 1871 on the ashes of the Schmidt Hotel at the southwest corner of Main and Madison Streets. *Missouri State Archives.*

State Penitentiary. He was elected Cole County's state representative in 1862 and the next year became editor of the *Missouri State Times*, which was named as the state's public printer.

Dr. Curry was involved in the library and building associations, railroad companies and Lincoln Institute's board of trustees. Soon after declaring bankruptcy in 1878, he moved to Texas.

William McCarty

Burr McCarty, who already had twenty-five years' experience operating his McCarty House, and his son, William G. McCarty, who had been proprietor of the Barnum Hotel in St. Louis, bought a five-year lease of the building and furniture from Curry & Burch. Unlike their cozy, homestyle McCarty House, the Hotel Madison was newly-furnished in first-class style.

When Governor B. Gratz Brown was nominated as the vice-presidential candidate on the Horace Greeley Democratic ticket in May 1872, a crowd gathered at the Hotel Madison, where the Jefferson City Brass Band played patriotic music, and then they marched to the Executive Mansion to celebrate Brown.

Burch, who also owned the *State Journal*, moved those offices into the Hotel Madison in August 1873, as well as his insurance agency and personal office.

Philip Cox, known for honesty and proficiency, had been the bartender at the Hotel Madison when, in November 1871, a woman arrived declaring him her husband. Mary Rulett said that they married in January and that she now had a child in St. Louis. Another woman showed up, claiming to have married him *eleven* years earlier and with *four* children. Cox was surprised by the second wife following him from St. Louis, but he was compelled to stay with the first and legal wife.

John Kaiser

In 1877, Dr. Curry defaulted on his loans and William McCarty closed the doors. At the time, the hotel had forty apartments and suites, a dining room to seat five hundred, a bar off, office, barber's saloon, a large storefront, and a spacious meeting hall.

In the spring of 1878, John Baptist Kaiser, manager of the City Hotel, agreed to lease the Hotel Madison with a formal grand opening in June. He renovated the place, changing the dining room to seating for one hundred with new furniture and china.

The renovated billiard room and bar included a "fine walnut counter" from Fred Binder's shop. The rooms had new carpets, marble-topped walnut furniture and beds with patent springs. The parlors all had gold-plated chandeliers and pianos.

Henry Barnes

In the kitchen were new appliances and pantries able to serve five hundred meals per day. Henry Barnes was chief cook for eight years. While chief cook at the City Hotel in 1874, Henry Barnes "filled it well, as the healthy and plump condition of the City Hotel boarders would indicate," the newspaper said. He learned his craft from his father, Howard Barnes, the city's first Black restaurant operator.

Particular about his kitchen, Henry Barnes once had an altercation with an ice delivery man. Barnes objected to a lump of ice being pulled across the kitchen floor from the door to the ice chest. When the delivery man argued, Barnes threw hot water in his face.

Henry Barnes provided food for community events, too. For example, the Independence Day grand picnic in 1884 was held at Franz Garden. A grand procession led from city hall to the garden, where the Declaration of Independence was read, string and cornet bands played, children's amusements were set up, and Barnes served barbecue. During the Democratic State Convention in 1880, the Hotel Madison kitchen served more than five hundred guests per day.

Frank James Surrenders

It is likely that outlaw Frank James stayed at the Hotel Madison the night after he surrendered to Governor Thomas Crittenden in October 1882. He had been induced to turn himself in after the murder of his brother, Jesse. Major John N. Edwards, a good friend of the outlaws from the Civil War days, was a newspaperman and also good friends with the McCarty family. He likely arranged the clandestine arrival in the Capital City. The night before the surrender, James used an alias in the hotel book at the McCarty House.

The next day, Frank James walked the town unrecognized and stopped into the capitol to arrange for his surrender, saying that he was repentant and reformed. The following day, James handed over his .44-caliber Remington revolver to Governor Crittenden.

That evening, nearly five hundred residents paraded through the Hotel Madison to greet the famous criminal, seated in his hotel room. Even Governor Crittenden and his wife stopped in during their evening stroll. "A stream of people of all sizes, ages and color…talked with the outlaw, while others were satisfied with simply looking at him a moment," according to Jean Carnahan's *If Walls Could Talk*.

John Kaiser Dual Leases

John Kaiser's lease of the Hotel Madison was set to expire in June 1883. A year before that, Kaiser bought the furniture and leased the City Hotel, operating both places simultaneously. "The major will have his hands full, but he is equal to the occasion, as no man in the state knows better how to 'keep hotel' than he does," the *Tribune* said.

The parlors of the Hotel Madison hosted many local organization meetings, as well as the statewide political party business and commission meetings. For example, in February 1883, local grocery men met and organized an association to protect their businesses from short weights and measures.

The Hotel Madison regularly hosted traveling performers as they passed through town. But in April 1883, Kaiser said that the Ford Opera Troupe was the last entertainment group he would take at any property. According to the *Daily State Journal*, the troupe refused to carry out the contract worked out by their agent.

Public Auction

The shareholders of the Hotel Madison held a sale in May 1883. The Jefferson City Real Estate Association bought the Hotel Madison for $15,000. Although Imperial Club leader Ashley Ewing made a bid to buy the hotel, where the social club held all of its events, the association

NEXT GENERATION

Ed J. Miller, described as clever and obliging, began as a clerk at the Hotel Madison in the spring of 1885. He would later become an owner. But at this time, he was an exceptional baseball player. For a time, he traveled with the Hastings Baseball Club out of St. Joseph, playing teams in Nebraska and Colorado. Miller was a "clever fielder, hard hitter and daring base runner," the *Tribune* said.

Kaiser visited his homeland of Baden in late 1886. He died in April 1887, just shy of his sixtieth birthday.

Kaiser's eldest son, Henry, who had been working for his father for seven years, took over the hotel operations. Two years later, Henry Kaiser was chief clerk of the Grand Windsor, the leading hotel in Dallas, Texas. Victor Kaiser remained as day clerk at the Hotel Madison, and Charles Kaiser began his work in hotels at age sixteen in 1890. He would continue at the Hotel Madison until his death in 1929.

sold to Kaiser two weeks later for $17,000 (about $500,000 in 2025 dollars).

Kaiser immediately began improvements inside and out. The *Daily State Journal* said of his work, "The Hotel Madison will henceforward be known as the most elegant hotel in the west." Among Kaiser's additions was an astronomical clock that showed the day of the month, hour of day, changes of the moon, position of the earth in relation to the sun, and signs of the zodiac.

The third annual meeting of the Ex-Confederates Association of Missouri required the Hotel Madison, as well as other hotels, to bring in extra cots and means to feed and lodge hundreds of visitors in August 1883. Future governor John Marmaduke was the association's president, and he hosted open-air concerts on the capitol grounds to benefit the Confederate cemetery in Springfield.

"During the presence of state conventions, it has been necessary to crowd several people in one room and to supplement the sleeping capacity of beds with cots, but the same thing has frequently to be done in St. Louis and Chicago," the *Tribune* said.

Many a political issue was discussed, and sometimes decided, in the parlors of the Hotel Madison. Such was the case in October 1883, when a committee of three was tasked with selecting the site for the new U.S. courthouse and post office. The decision was two for the Basye House/Fort Jackson site at the north end of Madison Street for $4,000 and one for the McCarty livery site near Jefferson Street on High for $6,000 (nearly $200,000 in 2025 value). Despite community approval of the site and the cost-savings at the Basye House, a few influential men caused the now-gone federal building to be installed on the livery site, across from the present post office on High Street.

In 1884, Kaiser renovated the two-story Imperial Club hall, adding sixteen guest rooms for a total of sixty-two and substituting a smaller reception hall.

With proximity to the Executive Mansion and the statehouse, the Hotel Madison often hosted distinguished visitors, who would be greeted by the public in its parlors. For example, Major General W.T. Clark of Washington, D.C., visited in January 1884 on official business as a federal revenue agent. A two-time Texas congressmen in the 1870s, Clark had begun his military service as adjutant general of the post in Jefferson City in 1861–62. In August 1886, Confederate General Joe Shelby stopped on a return trip to his farm in Adrian, meeting with friends and old soldiers past midnight.

Lobby Headquarters

In early 1887, both Sedalia and Boonville lobbied to relocate the capitol from Jefferson City to their communities, and both set up their operations in the Hotel Madison.

Organizations affiliated with state government or with statewide agendas also held their meetings in the Madison parlors. The modern form of the Missouri National Guard started with a group meeting of militia leaders from across the state in January 1897 to create a more organized military and to pursue state funding.

The Democratic State Convention in August 1888 again pressed the local hotels and boarding houses. Numbers showed the Madison, Central and Monroe with 250 guests each, City with 150 and McCarty with 75. The Craven House put up 30 and the Lansdown sisters 20.

The state's board of education and board of pharmacy met here, as did the statewide firemen seeking to establish a fund for disabled firefighters.

William K. Bradbury

William K. Bradbury bought the furniture from the Kaiser heirs and leased the building for ten years in the fall of 1888. Active in statewide Democrat politics, Bradbury was known for his energy and persistence, having been the deputy clerk of the Missouri Supreme Court for many years. Born in Morgan County, Bradbury came to Jefferson City when his father was employed as the prison deputy warden.

One of the first moves by the new owner was to have the hotel supplied with water from the new city waterworks. In the summer of 1889, Bradbury added a large sewer draining into the Missouri River. Bradbury then made architectural changes to the lower floor, including a new entrance and relocating the bar, office, and billiard parlor.

During the Grand Army of the Republic encampment of 1890, the Hotel Madison was headquarters to Mrs. Henrietta Wittenmeyer, national president of the National Woman's Relief Corps, the auxiliary to the men's organization chartered in 1883.

Ed J. Miller

Baseball player and sometime clerk Ed J. Miller took over in the fall of 1891 after only three years under Bradbury. One of his first changes was to upscale the billiard hall with four new tables and accessories.

Miller was born in Jefferson City and involved in many active groups, including hunting expeditions, golf, bowling tournaments, and particularly as pitcher of one of the city's best baseball teams. The fabled baseball team played an exhibition game at Cottage Place Park in 1886 with the St. Louis Browns team, which had just won the World Series.

The local athlete traveled with early bowling teams for tournaments with teams from Herman and Washington. Jefferson City had two clubs and two alleys—at Henry Wagner's Butchers & Drovers Saloon and Colonel Isaac Bodenheimer's Monarch Bar.

At the Hotel Madison in early 1892, graduates of what became the University of Missouri–Columbia met to organize an alumni association, open to graduates and former students, with newspaperman Henry W. Ewing as president. In September of that year, the World's Fair State Board met to ensure that the state had proper representation in Chicago.

Miller moved on in 1896 as an agent for Anheuser Beer, which had offices on Water Street near the depot until 1914.

MONROE HOUSE

1873–1926

The intersection of Monroe and High Streets is one of the most storied in the city, from favorite storefronts and iconic fires to city hall and the county courthouse. It also is one of the best preserved, with four historic, though not original, buildings as anchors. That includes the Monroe House.

William Maushund

The Maushund Saloon opened in 1867 near the northwest corner of Monroe and High Streets. William Maushund added a hotel in 1873, christened the Monroe House. Two years later, he added a restaurant "to keep pace with the times," the *Jefferson City Tribune* said.

Maushund was a bartender and caterer by trade and created a popular gathering place. Untold community events and issues passed through these early walls. For example, teenage deputy Peter Meyer walked from the South Side neighborhood to have a drink one morning in October 1876, after a dispute with his neighbor. That afternoon, he murdered carpenter Augustus Busekrus over a matter of pride.

Nearly all of the Monroe House windows were broken in a near-tornado windstorm that swept through the city in 1876. The unusually large hailstones, which claimed eighty-five window panes along High Street from the courthouse and city market house to Washington Street alone, also took out a thousand windows at the Missouri State Penitentiary.

A controversial veranda the length of the hotel on High Street was added in May 1876. Citizens were upset by the removal of a magnificent shade tree. By 1885, the veranda had become an eyesore and was removed.

The son of German-speaking immigrants who settled in Gasconade County, Maushund served three months in the Home Guard at Hermann then was a musician in the First Brigade band. He died in 1879 following injuries when the sleigh he was riding in overturned on Broadway. Doctors accidentally gave Maushund too much chloroform.

Billy Wagner

William "Billy" Wagner operated the Monroe House for twenty-five years. *Cole County Historical Society.*

Local brewer George Wagner bought the Monroe House and Maushund Saloon in August 1877 for $10,000 (about $300,000 in 2025 dollars). Born in Bavaria and trained as a printer, George Wagner benefited from the considerable property and business built by his father, Paulus. The City Brewery on Dunklin Street passed to George and his brother Christ in 1871. By 1878, the local brewery had become one of the largest in the state, rivaling St. Louis' Anheuser.

While George Wagner served as Cole County sheriff from 1878 to 1882, his son, William "Billy" Wagner, operated the Monroe House. Billy Wagner then followed his father as sheriff from 1882 to 1886.

Constant Improvements

The younger Wagner quickly gained a reputation for seeking the most modern conveniences to make his hotel "cozy and comfortable." Among Billy Wagner's first improvements was a new gong to call boarders to meals, which apparently rattled the neighbors' windows too. His next step was adding a twenty-four-by-seventy-foot dining hall that could seat up to ninety, serving the specialty of turtle soup.

Being across High Street from Bragg Hall, which hosted many community events and performances, it was an advantageous move, and he soon enlarged his saloon as well. "Under the management of Mr. W.W. Wagner, [the Monroe House] has grown in favor with the traveling public during the last year, until its register shows a list each day equal to that of the older and larger hotels," the *Tribune* said in 1883.

A three-story, seventy-five-foot addition along Monroe Street and one and a half stories added to the top of the original building were constructed in 1884. To build an adequate cellar, the solid rock had to be blasted out. "Explosions sent up timbers and pieces of stone into the air," the papers said. Afterward, the hotel boasted a fine barroom and billiard hall, as well as forty-three rooms.

The next year, the old section was remodeled inside with a new street entrance for ladies, larger rooms, and a wider hallway. Wagner also installed a Hess electric guest call and fire alarm system—only the second in the state. Buttons in the clerk's office could be touched individually or a lever controlled all at once to alert guest rooms. Guest rooms likewise had a small knob to indicate to the desk that they were up. "Wagner intends to keep ahead of the times when it comes to modern convenience," the newspaper said.

With his reputation as a caterer, many groups often scheduled dinners after their entertainment or meetings. The saloon lunch counter was so popular that he added a separate restaurant, a new kitchen, and a larger dining room. The menu in August 1886, for example, included lobster, softshell crabs, frog legs, clams, and fish.

Wagner made the Monroe House a leader in progress, especially with utilities. In September 1887, he lit his dining room with eight incandescent lightbulbs. The *Tribune* reported that the light was "quite brilliant and very pretty...[and] vastly superior to gas."

The Monroe House was opened in 1873 in conjunction with the Maushund Saloon. This is how it looked in 1891, when sketched by Frederick Suden. *Missouri State Archives.*

When the city was slow to introduce sewers, Wagner installed a private sewer from the hotel corner to the Missouri River down Monroe Street and allowed businesses along the way to connect in the summer of 1889. Afterward, the Monroe House guests had pure, fresh water in every room.

Then, in August 1891, the Jefferson City Light, Heat and Power Company laid its cable east as far east as the Monroe House. The entire house was rewired for electrical fixtures in April 1895, and two electric fans cooled the dining room that summer.

Blown Safe

Wagner was deputy sheriff in the spring of 1880 when the first case of safe-blowing occurred in Jefferson City. The targeted safe happened to be in his own saloon, despite his position and the proximity of the hotel across Monroe Street from the courthouse and jail.

The Monroe Street door to the saloon was found open after an employee and neighbors at the newspaper office heard a startling noise. It was "the boldest burglary decidedly" in the city, the newspaper said. An experienced burglar had drilled a hole in the steel plate safe door. Then the plaster of Paris filling the door was blown up with gunpowder.

The timing, around 1:00 a.m., aligned with Wagner being away, the saloon closed, and the porter at the depot awaiting new train arrivals. Local William Kelly was arrested, saying that a few strangers made him buy their train tickets west. He returned, but the strangers then blew up a safe in Tipton the next night.

Hub of Activity

The location of the Monroe House, at the busy intersection of Monroe and High Streets, gave it a front-row seat to many newsworthy events, from apprehending criminals and runaway buggies to parades and speeches.

In February 1887, Sheriff Wagner was called to the courthouse, where Judge Frederick A. Clarenbach was discovered lifeless, locked in the vault. Wagner was called to try to revive him. At the coroner's inquest, Wagner said that he had seen the judge in his hotel the day before looking dejected. Some months prior, Clarenbach had commented to Wagner that he wanted to "die with his boots on." Facing financial troubles, it was unlikely that Clarenbach's asphyxiation was accidental.

Many of the local clubs enjoyed the larger meeting space the Monroe offered, including the Templars, Masons, Owls, Germania, Pierian, Capital City Bicycle, and Capital Gun Clubs. Many of these benefited from Wagner's membership, like the Jefferson City Commercial Club, which was created in April 1893 in the parlors of the Monroe House, with a particular goal of seeing the Missouri River Bridge built.

Other organizations simply enjoyed the catering for their annual affairs, such as the Printers Annual Ball, held by the Typographical Union No. 119 on the anniversary of Benjamin Franklin's birth.

Dinners in conjunction with musicals and dances held in Bragg Hall, across High Street, were also popular at the Monroe House. The thoroughfare between the Monroe House and Bragg Hall further served as advertising and gathering space. In January 1886, Monsieur L.D. Ricardo of Philadelphia performed above the street by walking across a wire rope with his feet in baskets. And during the 1888 Harrison-Morton presidential campaign, Republicans hung a giant American flag from Bragg Hall to the Monroe House.

Wagner was polite, popular, and genial. When his father, George, died in 1895, the will left Billy the "privilege of purchasing the Monroe House for $20,000." His brothers Conrad and Lawrence had taken over the family brewery as C&L Wagner, Henry ran a bowling alley and saloon across High Street, Louis was a former county prosecuting attorney, and Christopher was a businessman in Sacramento, California.

While southern visitors and Democratic organizations headquartered at the Hotel Madison, Republicans and railroad leaders preferred the Monroe House. When construction of the Missouri River Bridge began in June 1895, W.A. Waldo of Leavenworth, Kansas, brought one hundred workers with him and made his headquarters at the Monroe House.

Looking to 1896, Wagner made plans for another addition and rebuild. The old two-story portion facing High Street was removed and replaced with architecture matching the newer part facing Monroe. By 1901, the latest updates were not at the caliber of the big-city hotels, but they were equal to any other in the state, the newspaper said.

Missing Pieces

Hotels often lost reusable items to attrition—silverware, linens, cups, and so on. But in October 1901, a search for two missing silver spoons from the Hotel Madison revealed nearly a wagonload of hotel goods from the Monroe. Lizzie Gibson, "Big Gip," had worked for three years at the Monroe House and just recently had begun work at the Scott House. Police entered a brick stable on Hog Alley, where Gibson made a home in one room, to find it "fairly jammed" with dishes, towels, silverware, glassware, napkins, bedsheets, and more from local hotels.

New Management

Victor Wagner, son of Billy, took over management of the four-story, forty-room Monroe House in 1902, leaving his interest in the Grand Union Hotel in St. Louis.

At about this same time, Republicans were searching for a new postmaster. Although they had many candidates, the selection committee specifically asked Billy Wagner, who said that he would not run but would serve if appointed, which he was. At the time, Wagner was president of the Jefferson City Light, Heat and Power Company and was a director for both the Jefferson City Water Works and the city Bridge and Transit Company.

A stock company was formed in May 1903 with plans to raze the existing Monroe House and replace it with a modern, four-story hotel stretching from High Street to the alley. Architects Miller & Opel designed a $75,000 plan for ninety rooms and a 1,500-seat opera house, which never materialized.

With the new telephone technology of 1903, the Monroe House once again showcased the latest technology by connecting live to a revival meeting in Warrensburg. The Bell Telephone Company placed a large transmitter near the pulpit, and a phone connection was opened to Jefferson City, where those in the Monroe parlor heard Reverend Wilson of Cincinnati, Ohio.

John Glutz became manager in 1904 after Victor Wagner accepted a job with the Missouri Pacific as a dining car conductor. Another son, Alfred Wagner, took over when Glutz married and moved to St. Louis. By its reopening in January 1, 1905, following a thorough renovation, son Henry Wagner, who had been manager of the Grand Union Hotel in St. Louis, was in charge.

Ernst Simonsen and Henry DeWyl

Local businessmen Ernst Simonsen and Henry DeWyl bought the property in May 1905. A serious remodel followed by contractor Henry Wallau, who was mayor at the time.

The long bragged-about restaurant on the Monroe Street side became DeWyl's one-hundred-by-twenty-five-foot drugstore, and the main floor sample room became the dining room. The front was refitted with glass and iron. A two-story, brick twenty-by-forty-three-foot addition was made to the rear along Monroe Street, which added sample rooms, sleeping rooms, and a kitchen. "Mr. Simonsen has done many things in Jefferson City to stir the pride of her citizens, but this is the most enterprising thing he has done thus far," the newspaper said.

That fall, Simonsen leased to T.O. Robinson, who previously operated the New Fulton Hotel. After only two years, Robinson went to California, and Henry DeWyl and Otto Newkom took over management.

James Houchin

James Houchin bought the Monroe House in the summer of 1909, with Henry F. Sarman as manager. Less than a year later, Houchin also bought the Hotel Madison. Several managers took their turn, until Jesse Palm, who also had the lease at the Hotel Madison, took over the lease at the Monroe in 1913.

Myrene Houchin Hobbs

The Monroe House was among several properties transferred to Myrene Houchin, daughter of James Houchin, in 1919 in the incorporation of Myrene Houchin Corporation, the first of its kind in central Missouri.

The longtime saloon of Felix Senevy on the first floor closed with Prohibition and was occupied by the Farmers and Mechanics Bank in 1920.

The Jack Hobbs Realty Company, owned by Myrene Houchin's husband, closed the hotel and converted the building into business offices in 1926. The earliest occupants were the local building and loan association, the Missouri-Kansas-Texas (MKT) Railroad offices, an optometrist, and

The Monroe House was converted into office space in 1926. *Missouri State Archives.*

Dallmeyer Insurance Company. The installation of a Millner passenger elevator in 1930 encouraged the leases for the forty rooms.

The building was restored in 1974 by Nicholas Monaco. Today, 235 East High Street offers leased office space as the Monroe Building.

CENTRAL HOTEL

1848–1969

The Central Hotel replaced the name Virginia Hotel at the northwest corner of Jefferson and High Streets when Joseph Huegel purchased the property from the heirs of Thomas Lawson Price in 1884. Huegel and his wife, Regina (Braun), had been managing the property for ten years already. As newlyweds, they operated the next-door Nichols House—she the house and he and bar. Two years later, they took over the Virginia Hotel, installing a new bar before opening on January 1, 1874.

Like other hotel operators during these crucial years of impressing the state to keep the Capitol in Jefferson City, Huegel continued making incremental improvements to the three-story, twenty-eight room hotel. In 1894, Huegel installed new bar fixtures, including a heavy carved oak bar, a

Joseph Huegel bought the Virginia Hotel and renamed it the Central Hotel, shown on the right, in 1874. *Missouri State Archives.*

sixteen-foot-long mirror, double mirrors on each side of the entrance, oiled hard maple floors, oak wainscoting, and a sideboard—all worked by local craftsman Henry Wallau.

New Central Hotel

The New Central Hotel opened in 1900 with a new High Street facade, a fourth floor and twenty new rooms, designed by Charles C. Opel and Company. The main entrance became an artistic vestibule with inlaid tile and large glass front windows, which replaced massive oak front doors and brought light in from High and Jefferson Streets.

The new French roof was covered with slate, floors were polished maple, Georgia marble was laid in bathrooms, a new stairway was constructed, and a dedicated space was made for a future elevator. Transoms were added above each room door for further light and ventilation.

The new stairway and banisters were carved oak; the hall and stairs were carpeted with red velvet. The large office hall opened into the barroom with

Right: Joseph and Regina (Braun) Huegel devoted decades to operating the Central Hotel. *Patrick Wilson.*

Below: A major renovation of the Central Hotel in 1899 added a fourth floor and new front. *Missouri State Archives.*

a semicircular counter of heavily carved oak. Behind it was the public parlor and cloakroom.

The second floor had private parlors and the ladies' bathrooms. Incandescent lights and gas were in most rooms, and all had electric call bells. Afterward, the fifty-by-sixty-foot hotel had 36 bedrooms and could accommodate up to 140 with folding beds in the parlors.

Only the basement dining room and kitchen were left untouched at this time. However, when a few farmers tried to enter the dining hall in their shirtsleeves, Huegel convinced them that it was still proper to wear their coats when dining at his hotel.

At the turn of the twentieth century, the Central Hotel was "considered one of the plushest hotels in Mid-Missouri," the *Daily Capital News* said.

A 1906 addition, designed by Miller and Opel and built by George Todd, included a fifty-by-ninety-nine-foot extension fronting Jefferson Street with five floors, adding forty-eight bedrooms and a large thirty-by-sixty-foot dining room. Sample and store rooms faced Jefferson Street, the reception area was enlarged, sixteen private baths were installed, and the elevator was added.

Now with seventy rooms, the Central Hotel was the largest in the city. At the same time, Huegel was the oldest hotelman in the city.

Joseph Huegel

Born in New Jersey to German-speaking immigrants, Huegel was a carpenter and teamster before working on his father's Cole County farm in 1869. He soon moved to town, becoming foreman of the harness factory at the Missouri State Penitentiary and then bartender for Joseph Glutz.

In the late 1870s, Huegel also partnered with Matias Wallendorf and Bernard Blume to build and operate the original Pacific Flouring Mill and sawmill on Wier's Creek north of Main Street. Blume previously had worked at G.H. Dulle's first mill on Jefferson Street.

Devoted Catholics, both Huegels were active in St. Peter Church and he served as treasurer of the Catholic Knights of America. Huegel also was elected Third Ward alderman.

Huegel purchased in 1913 the Nichols House, which stood between the Central Hotel and the U.S. Post Office. The next year, he was left a widower with seven adult children ages twenty-seven to thirty-nine.

New Mrs. Huegel

After traveling to Kansas City frequently for "business trips," Huegel sent a telegram in July 1915 to his family from Jackson, Missouri, that he had married Mary Walter. The second Mrs. Huegel had been matron of the Joseph Walter Home, an orphanage in Kansas City, for thirteen years with her sister Mrs. Julia Baker. She was described as a stately and tall woman with a "fine presence and winning personality." Born in 1881 on a farm in Wisconsin, the new Mrs. Huegel was younger than some of her stepchildren.

The second Mrs. Huegel established a tradition of celebrating Mr. Huegel's birthday in July 1916, inviting several old friends to surprise him. Then, in December 1916, Mrs. Huegel started another tradition of entertaining poor children for a Christmas dinner at the hotel. The new Mrs. Huegel supported a variety of charities, such as the local school for the blind and a factory in Jefferson City by ordering dozens of rugs for the hotel.

In 1917, the Huegels bought the first Packard in Jefferson City, of which Mrs. Huegel was the primary operator.

That same year, the Central Hotel incorporated, with 748 shares going to Joseph, 1 to Mary, and 1 to son Victor. Tracy & Swartwout, architects for the new capitol, redesigned the hotel office. However, Huegel preferred his piano stool over the fancy new desk chair.

In 1918, the basement front on Jefferson Street was enlarged and converted into an indoor garden. It became the Pagoda Garden with vine-covered arbors, tropical plants, and Japanese lanterns. Only soft drinks were served here, and when World War I soldiers returned, it was a popular stop for sweethearts. The Huegels soon expanded the dance floor, and it became a central gathering place.

The first-of-its-kind cafeteria was opened at the Central Hotel in late 1919. The new food service method had gained popularity in larger cities. Then a cut stone pillar portico was added to the front of the Central Hotel in 1920.

The year 1924 marked Joseph Huegel's fiftieth anniversary working in hotels. It was a topic of hotel magazines across the nation, including the *Hotel World*, *Tavern Talk* and the *National Hotel Reporter*. This year, another remodel added twenty rooms, just in time for the Capitol Dedication Day in October. Mrs. Huegel prepared for three thousand guests, including one thousand chickens from their farm near today's Memorial Park.

Within three years after Mary Huegel took over the primary responsibilities, the hotel had cleared its indebtedness and grown from $25,000 to $150,000 annual gross income. Her focus was on the dining experience and popularizing the hotel as an assembly space. Many of the conventions that booked the Central Hotel were of a religious or social nature, as opposed to the political groups using the Madison and Monroe Hotels.

Successful in a business led by men, Mary Huegel gained attention for her "remarkable success," among those attending the Missouri-Kansas-Oklahoma Hotel Men's Association convention in 1927. "Hotel keeping, after all, is only housekeeping and homemaking on a large scale, so why should it not be the province of the womanly woman, as well as of a business man?" the newspaper proposed. In particular, Mary Huegel's talents were in her famous meals, mostly supported with produce from her own farm.

Growing up on a Wisconsin farm, she knew how to manage a diverse range of produce. In addition to the traditional vegetable garden, she kept berry bushes, grapevines, and apple and plum orchards. She raised three thousand chickens, served her own eggs, and produced more than forty-five thousand pounds of pork from Duroc-Jerseys and Poland-Chinas. "Developing my farm means more to me than traveling Europe. It has not all been easy, but hardships have been fine training. I never enjoy defeat—in fact, I refuse to accept it," Mary Huegel told the newspaper.

Family Lawsuit

Joseph Huegel died in 1926, never realizing his lifelong dream to manage a 250-room establishment. He had operated the same property for fifty-two years, the longest of anyone in Jefferson City.

Mary was defendant in a suit by the children of Joseph Huegel's first wife, Regina. She won sole control of the Central Hotel in late 1927. But in 1930, she lost the fight to maintain a majority stock in the Central Hotel Company after the six children gained the majority.

The Huegel estate—including the hotel, two city lots, and twenty-one acres on the California Road—was sold at a sheriff's sale in 1933 to the Jefferson City Realty Company for $1,500 (only $36,400 in 2025 dollars).

Louis Rose and Leo Levy

Owners Louis Rose and Leo Levy of Kansas City planned to raze the historic structure and replace it with a modern version in 1937. They had been

The Central Hotel was claimed by the state and razed in 1969. *Missouri State Archives.*

leasing since 1929 and bought the property in 1933. As early as 1935, the state was eyeing the corner property. The Capitol Commission had designed the new Capitol Park with the idea that all structures would be removed between Capitol and High and Jefferson and Broadway.

The hotel was almost claimed by fire in 1940 when a guest fell asleep with a lit cigarette. Newspapermen Charles Fear and Harry Edwards credited the second Mrs. Huegel's "persistent insistence" to install a sprinkler system decades earlier with its survival.

Mike Michelson

Rose partnered with Reuben "Mike" Michelson in 1943. Michelson had been with the Central Hotel since 1928 and part-owner since 1940. Michelson became manager in 1946 and sole owner in 1957. Born in 1907, Michelson was the son of immigrants from Latvia and Austria. Michelson moved to Jefferson City after his father was murdered in St. Louis.

The property was sold in 1964 to Helen M. O'Brien of St. Louis. In 1966, Michelson, still manager, voluntarily closed the hotel, unable to keep it adequately staffed.

State Capitol Park

Talk of a new high-rise hotel circulated in 1967, but the state, led by John Paulus Jr., director of state planning and construction, still wanted that land. The state paid $321,000 (about $3 million in 2025 dollars) for it, with additional plans to demolish the old post office, to complete the "open air concept" of the Capital Park. After its many variations over 120 years, the Virginia turned Central Hotel was razed in 1969.

Part VII

1880 to 1899

In 1880, the city's hotels could accommodate nearly 1,700 guests, including 460 at the Madison, 300 at the Tennessee House, 240 at the City Hotel, 225 at the Central Hotel, 175 at the Monroe House, 150 at the McCarty House, and 120 at the Neef Hotel. Several smaller hotels and boarding houses were also thriving, including the Pacific and Nichols Hotels and boarding houses of Joe Zuber at 212 Madison Street, Mrs. Howe on High, and the Lansdown sisters on Madison.

"Sedalia is coming down in a body to camp with us 'til the Capital is removed and then take it back with them. We welcome the gentlemen with open arms. We have plenty of good hotels and boarding houses that would profit by their visit—we have also plenty of good fresh water to astonish their innerds with," the *Tribune* said in 1881.

Another building boom blessed the city in the early 1880s. The newspaper called 1882 the most prosperous in the city's history up to that point.

Built of brick, stone, and iron, these new buildings expressed a sense of permanence in their architecture. The thousands of dollars spent within a brief time is a testament to the investment individuals were willing to make, ensuring that the capital remained.

Most hotels included a bar, but they had plenty of competition. According to 1884 dramshop licenses, John P. Raithel paid the highest fees, operating his West End Saloon, and Billy Wagner at the Monroe House was second. Close runners for third were Kaiser's Madison and City Hotels, as well as independent saloons of John G. Schott, C. Vetsburg, Frank Hoerschen, H.B. Holley, Henry Wagner, and C. Speedy. Saloons with lesser revenue included

Joseph Huegel's Central Hotel followed by the independent bars of Isaac Bodenheimer, E. Hoechstadter, Ernst Freimel, and Henry Falk.

Hotels and boarding houses all featured restaurants or dining rooms at the time. In June 1886, this capacity was pushed to its maximum when a St. Louis excursion brought nearly three thousand visitors to the capitol, Missouri State Penitentiary, and Jefferson City National Cemetery. While many stayed for lodging, all required meals.

A few dined with friends, but most formed lines to wait for tables at the local hotels and independent restaurants. The Hotel Madison served 670, the Monroe 550, and the City Hotel 500. Central Hotel served 350 and the Tennessee House 240. The independent restaurants of Howard Barnes' Delmonico and Joseph Zuber served 200 and 125, respectively. Even the Neef Hotel and the McCarty House served 75 between them.

When the ninth annual statewide GAR encampment came to Jefferson City in April 1890, "The hotels [were] taxed to their utmost capacity both in the matter of feeding and caring for guests," the *Tribune* said. The Madison, City, Monroe and Central Hotels reduced their fares to $1.50 per day and boarding houses even smaller rates. Cots were set up in public halls, and many participants brought their own tents. Meals were still provided to all visitors at an agreed upon cost of $0.35 (about $12.00 in 2025 dollars).

Free postal mail delivery was introduced in early 1890 under Postmaster William McCarty. Further revealing the central nature of hotels to the community's everyday life, five large mail collection boxes were placed at the Hotel Madison, City Hotel, and Monroe House, as well as at the corners of Main and Lafayette and High and Jefferson Streets. Another fifteen smaller boxes were installed across town.

Further community developments in the late 1880s included the opening of a city waterworks, the installation of the streetcar, and the enlargement of the Capitol.

Farmers Home

1880–1918

While the earliest hotels centered on the capitol and the biennial elected visitors, a few post–Civil War hotels emerged for the benefit of area farmers bringing their produce to the mill or market. The South Side hotels of

Thanksgiving Dinners

Hoteliers went all out for Thanksgiving dinners, which were community affairs during this era. For example, the Hotel Madison menu in 1889 included:

Saddle rock oysters raw, with sliced lemon and celery
Soup: Cream tomato, beef broth
Relishes: Olives, celery, cranberry sauce, chow chow, sweet peach pickle, tomato catsup, spiced pickles
Fish: Baked trout, anchovy sauce, Saratoga chips, baked red snapper, egg sauce, mashing potatoes
Boiled ham in champagne sauce
Tongue in orange jelly
Roast loin beef in brown gravy
Stuffed pig and applesauce
Baked turkey with fried oysters
Game: Stuffed quail in drawn butter, baked possum with sweet potatoes
Salads: Chicken, cabbage
Vegetables: Cream potatoes, sweet corn, escalloped tomatoes, French peas
Pastry: Mince pie, pumpkin pie, cocoanut layer cake, banana cake, Prince Wales cake, fig cake, pineapple cheese, crackers
Dessert: Wine jelly, whipped cream, orange ice, vanilla ice cream, mixed nuts, raisins, malaga grapes, bananas, oranges
Wine, black coffee, salted almonds

That same year, William and Alena (Bohrer) Wagner, served at the Monroe House:

Blue points on half shell with celery
Boiled red snapper in lobster sauce
Baked bluefish, maître d'hotel
Leg of mutton, a la jardiniere
Boned turkey with cranberries
Cold slaw
Breast of young Bremen goose in aspic jelly
Potato salad
Ribs of premium beef with browned potatoes
Haunch of venison with currant jelly
Young turkey with almond dressing
Sugar corn
Mashed potatoes
Butter beans
Tenderloin of beef with larded mushrooms
Chicken croquets with French peas
Choice asparagus on toast
Pickles gherkins horseradish
Worcestershire sauce, tomato catsup
Lemon meringue pie, mince pie, peach pie, English plum pudding, rum sauce
Orange ice, wine jelly, assorted cakes, coconut cake, angel food cake, fruit cake, mixed nuts, fruit, Edam and cream cheese
Rhine wine, claret, Mosell, Mumm's extra dry, Piper Heidsieck
Coffee, tea, milk

"Jefferson City is proud of its hotels and of the enterprise of their managers. More than most people realize, they are an important factor in building up the old town and extending its popularity. Their managers are men of affairs. They work in harmony and are among the best-known men in Missouri," the *Republican Review* said.

Entertainment

Lack of entertainments was one of the many accusations flung at the Capital City as reasons the capitol ought to be relocated. Many ventures over the decades came and went to address that issue. Almost always, a local hotel was participant, if not host, of these endeavors. Billiards, baseball, bowling, musical concerts, picnics, and even roller skating were among the list.

The city's first performance hall was half of the fourth floor of Schmidt's Hotel, which was lost to fire in 1871. Then the replacement Hotel Madison included a ballroom, often occupied by the Imperial Club, which organized large-scale dances and balls for the social elite.

A little later, Henry Bragg built Bragg's Hall on East High Street. Here the community saw traveling shows and performers, like Jenny Lind and Ole Bull. But it was also the gathering place for local thespians, musical shows, and school programs. Bragg Hall also was lost to fire.

Joseph Clark built an odd performance hall above his livery stable on the north side of the 300 block of Main Street, about where First Christian Church is today.

Then Louis Lohman fulfilled a long-held dream of opening an eight-hundred-seat opera house near the capitol. The location required the removal of the historic Jefferson House, opened by the Curry family. It was built next to the mercantile of Lohman's father, Charles. The first performance in the three-story, Victorian-style Lohman Opera House, 102–104 East High Street, was October 5, 1886—the vaudeville show of *Bob and Zip*, starring Patti Rosa.

Farmers Home and Nieghorn House were different from the uptown hotels in many regards, from German-speaking hosts and food to wagon yards to care for horses and produce.

The German-speaking area of the South Side had developed on the south side of Wier's Creek, separate but within walking distance of the original uptown. The Farmers Home, at the southeast corner of Jefferson and Dunklin Streets, became an anchor of the self-sustaining neighborhood. Tanner's general store and machine shop was across Jefferson Street and

Another major contributor to capital retention was the Imperial Club and its social season. The group of young gentlemen, mostly of southern heritage, hosted parties at large homes, river excursions, picnics, and dances at the local halls. They began as early as 1870, and while they first met at Harmonie Hall, their headquarters for the last decades of the nineteenth century was at the Hotel Madison. The newspapers covered their events in detail, even listing each attendee and his or her disguise for masquerade balls, and how crowds of the uninvited gathered outside the venue to see what the "high-toned gentlemen [and] elite ladies" would wear to these "metropolitan gayeties."

Not only was the design to provide entertainment for the select few locals, but it would also occupy the visiting elected officials and persuade them that Jefferson City was the best place for the capitol to remain. As the Imperial Club gained influence, leaders were accused of marrying off Jefferson City's daughters to visiting bachelors in exchange for goodwill for the city. The Imperial Club even took charge of inaugural balls for several governors.

When John Kaiser remodeled the Hotel Madison in 1878, the Imperial Club's events found their home. The improved hall on the second floor of the hotel was "one of the best halls for dancing purposes in the state" and featured a new chandelier lit with gas. Then an 1884 renovation created dressing rooms with the hall.

"If it were not for the Imperial Club, Jefferson City would be as dead socially as it is in every other respect," the *Glasgow Journal* once said.

Morlock's provisions across Dunklin. The fourth corner was Schwartze's blacksmith shop.

For the area farmers coming to town, this intersection was essential to make the overnight trip, exchange their goods for provisions they needed, and to do any other business they needed during the short stay. Farmers and their families often visited the South Side over the weekends, with the Farmers Home providing a center of socializing and entertainment. In nineteenth-century German culture, it was a *gasthaus*, or guest house.

A beer saloon operated by John and Barbara Opel in a frame building opened on this prominent corner about 1858. Then Joe Haas operated the saloon through the 1870s, with live music on a wooden stage for dance parties in the backyard.

In 1880, Jacob Schmidt renovated the space as a farmers and drovers home. The newspaper said that it "will be one of the snuggest and most pleasant hostelries in the state." A "big-hearted host," Schmidt held a grand opening in October 1880, complete with a "sumptuous lunch and musical entertainment" under a new outdoor pagoda.

Jacob Schmidt

Before coming to Cole County about 1864, Schmidt had been a teacher in Indiana. He farmed on the Moreau River, where he filled several icehouses each winter to sell in the following summer, earning the nickname "Moreau Ice Bear."

Schmidt also was active in the Democratic Party and through the 1880s was manager of the Annual Harvest Festival, put on by Cole County farmers on the Moreau. In 1883, the event included a forty-by-sixty-foot dance floor, Freimel's string band, an old-fashioned basket dinner, and a twenty-entry colt show.

As a community anchor, the Farmers Home often was the first stop for German-speaking immigrants while they found a place to settle in the area.

John Asel took over the site in 1887, earning a reputation as a popular host of guests and social events. That same year, he was the county jailer and broke his ankle jumping from a train. He then broke his leg two years later when he was thrown from a wagon. Asel was a merchant in Brazito and then Bass, where he also was postmaster. Sadly, after a "fit of insanity" in 1912, he shot himself twice in the head.

In 1889, Fred "Fritz" Truetzel of Osage City bought the hotel. He was the county public administrator at the time. At the Farmers Home, Truetzel stepped up the quality of meals and liquor. He later bought the Pacific House on Monroe Street.

Two years later, George "Caspari" Bassmann, who farmed for more than thirty years in the county, bought the property.

Nick Kielman

After the frequent change of hosts, the Farmers Home was purchased in February 1894 by Cole County–born Nick Kielman. For nearly a decade, Kielman and partner Benjamin Humbrock operated the hotel. Kielman and Humbrock were well-known huntsman and caterers as well. Their table often included raccoon, 'possum, turkey, quail, squirrel, and rabbit from their own hunting trips. For example, at the celebration of the reopening in 1897, they served a 'possum feast.

Kielman was easily spotted by his white felt Stetson hat with a sweeping brim when out. A popular brick worker and bartender, Humbrock was even named grand marshal of the Labor Day Parade in 1903.

New Farmers Home

The building seen today was built in 1897 by property owner Jacob Tanner. The *fachwerk*-style building included two staircases to the guest rooms from Jefferson and from Dunklin Streets. The New Farmers Home was noted for having liquor by the gallon, substantial meals, and comfortable rooms. Kielman's lunch counter was known for its hot tamales and pretzels.

The second story of the brick structure had nineteen sleeping rooms; the main floor saloon is today's ECCO Lounge. The kitchen and dining room were in the basement, where daily meals were served to about thirty guests and locals were seated at two long tables. "This old-world, country style of communal eating contrasted with service elsewhere in the city," local historian Walter Schroeder said.

The Italian floor tiles still seen today at ECCO Lounge were installed by Kielman in about 1906, when Kielman bought the entire building.

Kielman was known for having a menagerie on display from time to time, including a monkey from the Philippine Islands, where his son served in the military; a catamount shot on a nearby farm; and a five-foot rattlesnake he killed in a local creek.

The corner was the site of festive dances and traveling entertainment. "It was hands down the entertainment center for the German-speaking South Side," Schroeder said. But it also saw tragedies, such as three of nine children of the Charles Hardin family, traveling from Savannah, dying of measles there in 1910.

This is the Jefferson Street entrance to the Farmers Home saloon, provided by Jack Howser. *Walter Schroeder.*

After nearly fifty years as a wagon lot, hotel, and restaurant, the Farmers Home closed in July 1918. Afterward, rooms were rented to "permanent guests." The restaurant closed, but the saloon business continued until Prohibition closed its doors. "No commercial building better embodies the essence of the Munichburg community in both its longstanding centrality to the neighborhood and in its architecture than the Farmers Home building," Schroeder said.

The Farmers Home also had a five-stepped cave for cold storage in the hillside and a hand-dug tunnel under Jefferson Street, supposedly to connect to the nearby brewery. "County farmers would bring their moonshine and home brew to Farmers Home and sell it in the basement," Schroeder said.

Kielman's heirs sold in 1937 on the courthouse steps after foreclosure. Long-term guest rooms became apartments, and a bakery occupied the former restaurant in the basement. The saloon reopened as Farmers Café under Leonard Weaver and then as Emma's Tap Room, owned by Emma "Big Em" Haulenbeek. The name ECCO ("Earl Childers Construction Company") was added in 1945 by Earl and Kay Childers. The property continues to operate today as the city's "oldest restaurant and lounge."

NIEGHORN HOUSE

1892–1923

After completion of his journeyman tailor requirements and his military obligations in Bavaria, John Neighorn immigrated in 1848 to Cole County. In addition to amassing more than one thousand acres in the Zion area south of Jefferson City, he and his sons operated an early distillery, horse mill, and sawmill. Family records suggest that he also operated a trading post and continued to make handkerchiefs and pantaloons, which he would trade for other goods with Lohman-Maus at the city landing. He also was known to be a lender for new immigrants getting started.

After his wife, Anna Margaret (Schubert, widow Kiesling), died in 1888, Nieghorn moved into a farmhouse, with land and barns, at 114 East Dunklin Street. In 1892, he built a rooming house next door to his home at 120 East Dunklin Street. Popular builder Henry Wallau did the design and brick work, while John's son Andreas Nieghorn quarried the

John Nieghorn built the Nieghorn House in 1892 on the south side of Dunklin Street between Madison and Jefferson. *Gary Schmutzler.*

John Nieghorn opened the Nieghorn House in the South Side neighborhood in 1892. *Thomas Fales.*

limestone from the family farm south of town and laid it. Advantageously, gas and water lines had just reached Dunklin Street when the Nieghorn House was completed.

When the sign painter ran out of room, family legend says, the *g* was dropped, creating an iconic misspelling on the east side of the new brick building—*Niehorn* House. The name also had the problem of English speakers reversing the vowels, creating the misspelling of the bridge south of town—*Neighorn* Branch Bridge.

Fred Sessinghaus

Fred Sessinghaus, an intelligent and industrious German-speaking immigrant, leased the property and business from Nieghorn. He was well liked and admired for not being afraid to "take hold of an enterprise," the local newspaper said.

John Nieghorn lived in the hotel with his grandson John T. Nieghorn until his death in 1899. In addition to rent, Sessinghaus provided a meal and pail of beer each evening.

Registration for a room at the Nieghorn House was made in the restaurant, which included the saloon, on the first floor. The other side of the building's first floor initially was leased by harness maker Louis Sachs. Between the two retail spaces, there was a center staircase to the second and third floors. Similar to the Farmers Home, the Nieghorn House also offered a livery, wagon yard, and scale. The rooms could be rented by the day or hour, and a variety of services were said to be provided by the maids.

In its early days, the Nieghorn House saw tremendous business from area farmers.

Fatal Gas

Many hotels faced near-death, and a few fatal, experiences for guests unfamiliar with the new gas lighting technology. The gas had to be turned off to extinguish the light, rather than blowing out the flame, as one would with a candle. The result of leaving the gas on without a flame to consume it was a lack of oxygen in an enclosed room and eventual asphyxiation.

In mid-December 1894, a pair of Hickory Hill brothers were victims of the new technology. Both were found motionless on the bed with the unmistakable odor of gas in the room. Moved to a room with clean air, they were examined by physicians. The older brother, Roe Scott, forty-five, was dead, leaving a wife and five children. Walter Scott, thirty-eight, was larger and had strong lungs, which likely helped him survive. The Scotts had come to town with their produce and then enjoyed themselves in the saloon before retiring at about 2:00 a.m.

The fatal incident left a lasting effect on what otherwise was a promising business. Sessinghaus closed the bar in February 1895 and returned to his carpentry business.

Frank Stockman and John Stockman, orphaned brothers from Wardsville, leased the Nieghorn House next. They held grand balls, turkey lunches, and fish fries open to guests and the community. Inside, Henry Schneider built a bowling alley in late 1896. But the Stockman brothers sold the business back to John Nieghorn in 1898, perhaps due to a lawsuit earlier that year where a wife sued for $1,000 and forfeiture of their liquor license for violating the 1889 dramshop laws and serving her husband.

Robbery Gone Wrong

Mrs. Eliza Markham was in charge of the hotel in November 1899 when traveler Ed F. Gilmore was found dead in suspicious circumstances in the doorway of an outhouse, face down with his hat, coat, and shoes laying neatly inside. Liquor bottles and an empty morphine bottle were found.

Dirt and feathers showed that the body had been dragged from a nearby house, owned by Maude Miller and May "Morphine May" Salzer, who were considered of poor character.

Gilmore was stopping in Jefferson City, driving his wagon from Camden County back to Columbia. Witnesses eventually revealed that he was overdosed accidentally with morphine after being given chloroform to be robbed of more than $100. For the murder, Miller was acquitted and Salzer was sentenced to two years in the Missouri State Penitentiary, but both were indicted for grand larceny.

Ben Hoffmeyer

Bernard Hoffmeyer took charge of the Nieghorn House in December 1900, after it had sat vacant for some time. He kept horse teams associated with the house and sent drummers into the country to advertise. Hoffmeyer emigrated as a child from France, was a farmer in Moniteau County, and served during the Civil War in the Cole County Home Guard and then Company G of the Tenth Cavalry.

One storeroom was converted into a butcher shop when Fred Scheinert brought his business from California, Missouri. Another storeroom was turned into a gymnasium for the local Modern Woodmen of America club. The front retail space became a general store with goods and groceries moved by B.E. Garrison and his father, Robert, who also relocated from California, Missouri. Lastly, the other retail space became Ernest Buerhle's barbershop after he split business with his brother, John, on High Street.

South Side Hotel

George "Caspari" Bassmann took over the business in June 1901 and bought the building from Andreas Nieghorn in 1903, changing the name to "South Side Hotel." Briefly, Bassmann had operated the Farmers Home. Then he partnered with John Sommerer in 1897 to take over the grocery business of Lawrence Wagner on High Street.

The commercial block on Dunklin Street grew in 1908 when brothers John Schmidt and Henry Schmidt opened a shoe store to the west and a grocery store to the east of the South Side Hotel.

Bassmann leased the hotel to Adam Schneider and August Raithel in 1911. Schneider was a veteran bartender, having worked at several hotel bars, and was a longtime officer in the local Bartender's Union. Raithel worked at the nearby brewery. Later, Louis Jacobs leased the business, closing his Oyster Bay restaurant on Madison Street.

Bassmann Apartments

In 1923, Bassmann converted the upper levels into eight efficiency apartments, while the first floor remained retail space. The Bassmann Apartments featured Murphy beds and a window to the hallway for ice delivery, South Side historian Walter Schroeder said.

Unlike many of the early uptown hotels, the Nieghorn House and Farmers Home remain and contribute to the Munichburg Historic District, as listed in the National Register of Historic Places. The Nieghorn House Bassmann Apartments were restored in 2010 and continue to operate as commercial and residential.

NEEF HOUSE

1884–1937

Baden-born tinsmith Herman Henry Neef opened the Neef House at 105 West High Street in 1884. He and his wife, Mary (Brenneisen), were no strangers to the hospitality industry.

Herman Neef was a Baden immigrant, Civil War veteran, tinsmith, and hotel operator. *Cole County Historical Society.*

This forty-four-room, brick house was built about 1862. Owned by Joseph Heinrichs, it was a gathering place for social events, like the city Music Society. In the 1870s, it was the home of Horace B. Johnson, who was elected Missouri attorney general in 1869 and argued cases before the federal and state Supreme Courts until 1877.

Mrs. Howe used the Empire-style property as a boarding house for about seven years, before the Neefs. This hill likely was the location of the first City Hotel as well.

Herman Neef

Herman Neef's father had been a wealthy and prominent hotel operator in Baden before being forced to flee in 1848 after the failed German Revolution. Neef studied at a Swiss Lyceum and was trained as a tinner. He came to Jefferson City from St. Louis after his mother died, working in the hardware store of Andreas Gundelfinger.

He and his brother Isidor opened a tin and sheet iron manufactory on Madison between Main and High Streets in 1856. But in the summer of 1859, they defaulted on a loan and had to sell their forty-nine-by-twenty-six-foot, two-story brick home and shop, as well as their tools.

The brothers then opened a stove and tinware dealership in Tipton, later adding stores in Sedalia, Warrensburg, and Versailles. Over the years in Tipton, Neef was elected to the school board and city council and as city treasurer.

During the Civil War, Neef was a sergeant in Company H of the Cole County Home Guards and then commissioned a lieutenant of Company G in the Forty-Second Enrolled Missouri Militia. Afterward, he was among the 134 charter members of the Garfield GAR Post in Jefferson City.

A wealthy merchant in 1868, Neef opened a brewery in Tipton that was lost to fire. He then built a large frame hotel in Tipton, which also burned along with one-third of the town. Then, he moved back to Jefferson City.

In 1874, Neef opened the Neef House at 208 Madison Street, where the former Hannegan home had been renovated as a hotel, with a bar in the front room. The day before the December opening, Neef shot himself in the stomach while cleaning his gun at the bar. He survived, although initially they were so confident it was fatal that they sent for Father Miller for confession.

The *California Democrat* described him as "a kind and obliging host and a good citizen."

After less than two years, he took charge of the former Wagner Hotel, refitting it in May 1876 as the Neef House and saloon at 131 High Street. Here he was known for keeping a "menagerie" in cages and aquariums, including prairie dogs, rabbits, squirrels, and canaries. This Neef House was closed in February 1881 by building owner George Wagner due to unpaid rent.

Herman Neef opened the Neef House at 105 West High Street in 1885. Neef Terrace was added in front in 1897. *Missouri State Archives.*

Suffering from rheumatism and a long run of excessive use of liquor, Neef attempted suicide by stabbing himself just below the heart with a three-inch bladed jackknife, saying, "I want to see Jesus." Once recovered, Neef moved to Tuscumbia, where he opened another tinsmith shop. He then bought a team and wagon to transfer travelers from the Aurora Springs railroad station to Tuscumbia.

By 1883, Neef had returned again to Jefferson City, this time as landlord of the Tennessee House. But Sheriff William Wagner soon took Neef, defined as "slightly deranged," to St. Vincent Asylum in St. Louis for several months.

Upon his return, Neef also manufactured lightning rods, hosted community picnics, and opened a tinware store on West Main Street. Always ready to try the next thing, Neef also organized the Jefferson City Prospecting Company after gold was reported near Guthrie.

New Neef House

One of the first things Neef did after buying Mrs. Howe's boarding house in 1884 was install a beautiful zinc fountain in front of the New Neef House. A fire in the summer of 1888 south of the Neef House on Jefferson, at Victor Zuber's old two-story frame home, threatened both the Neef House and Paul Schmidt's wagon shop to the south. Afterward, the Neef House added a third story with a tin roof constructed by Neef.

In 1897, Frank Miller built Neef Terrace, two store rooms and four modern flats, at street level and in front of the Neef House. The family continued to operate the Neef House and Terrace after his death in 1900, until it was sold in 1937. While the grand home is gone and the hillside razed, the Neef Terrace remains part of the downtown streetscape, adjacent to the historic Merchants Bank building, built about 1889.

Craven House

1895–1906

A short-lived hotel, the Craven House offered twenty-four furnished rooms at 311 Monroe Street beginning in about 1895. Grocer John T. Craven built the hotel next door to the family home at 305 Monroe Street just a few years before his death. The location had been the horse lot of federal judge Robert Wells in the city's early years.

Craven was born in Pennsylvania, served four years as a major in the Civil War, married into the local Gundelfinger family, and operated businesses in Jefferson City for thirty years. He was business partner early in his career with other notable businessmen, including S.C. Scovern, Charles Thomas, and William Q. Dallmeyer. His grocery store relocated several times uptown, twice due to fires. After Craven's death in 1895, the Craven Grocer and Produce Company became the Burch-Mason-Berendzen Grocer Company.

Even the Craven House was damaged by one of the business fires that began at the southeast corner of High and Monroe Streets. It was "one of the biggest and most damaging fires that has occurred in Jefferson City in many years," the newspaper said. A young employee was sent to the basement to fill a container with gasoline. However, he dropped the candle he was using for light into the can; flames from the basement were then fanned by strong winds.

Louisa (Gundelfinger) Craven continued to operate the Craven House, with a reputation of special rates for theatrical troupes and excellent Easter dinners. Louis Bosse briefly leased the house from 1897 to 1899.

Bybee House

Elwood T. Bybee of Fulton bought the furniture and leased the Craven House in March 1901, allowing Mrs. Craven to move to St. Louis. He changed the name to the Bybee House.

An eighteen-year-old woman from Brumley was assistant cook at the Bybee House in February 1902 when she gave birth to a healthy boy in her room. She then walked from her room on the second floor to a window, where she dropped the newborn to the ground. She was found in her room by a coworker complaining of cramps, so Bybee called for a doctor. When Bybee went to the woman's door, he heard a baby's cry. The doctor found her in the closet, and police heard the baby's cry on the ground. The child survived but a few days, and then the mother was charged with murder.

The following month, Bybee returned to his farm in Callaway County. John Suggett of New Bloomfield bought the furnishings and lease. Conrad Waldecker then bought the building from Mrs. Craven and the furniture and fixtures from Suggett.

Normandie Hotel

Mrs. Craven had moved in 1901 to St. Louis, where she kept a boarding house, taking advantage of the guests drawn to the World's Fair. Afterward, she purchased back the Jefferson City property and renamed it the Normandie Hotel. By July 1906, she sold for the last time. Her "gracious nature endeared her to intimate acquaintances," the newspaper said upon her death one year later in St. Louis.

New Hotel Madison

1869–1939

The Hotel Madison entered a new era in June 1896 when the Kaiser estate and Ed Miller sold both the property and the lease to Bernhard "Ben" G. Vieth, who had been co-owner of the City Hotel. Kaiser sons Victor and Charles remained as clerks.

Immediately, Vieth papered the interior, added electric fans to the club rooms, installed tile flooring, and added steam heat in advance of the Democratic State Convention that August.

By the end of that year, the nostalgic old wood stove at the center of the Hotel Madison lobby was replaced with a more modern heating system. At the passing of the nostalgic artifact, the *Kansas City World* said, "Few politicians in the state have not spit on it at one time or another."

Ben Vieth

Vieth's true passion was music, and he participated in a variety of local musical organizations over the decades. In 1880, he was an original member of the Jefferson City Cornet Band, serving as treasurer and playing the B-flat. In 1892, he used his influence to bring the Southwest Missouri Band Association Conference to Jefferson City. At the time, it had seventeen member bands from Hermann to Carthage, and Theodore H. Haar, its musical director, was from Jefferson City.

Ben Vieth bought the Hotel Madison from the Kaiser family estate in 1896. *Missouri State Archives.*

Vieth was involved with the Missouri River Bridge development committee in 1893 with fellow hotelier Billy Wagner. Not surprisingly, when it was time for the big bridge dedication in May 1896, Vieth was on the music committee.

When twenty-one men organized a Jefferson City Street Fair Association in 1899, he was among them and helped solicit more donations. At the Great Horse Show of 1899 at Cottage Place Park, Vieth had the exclusive liquor license.

Vieth was also among the local visionaries hoping for urban railways to connect Missouri's cities. And he was among the first to purchase an automobile from Theodore Burkhardt, ordering a Thomas Macknies in 1908.

When the first ninety-five men organized the Jefferson City Country Club under Governor Herbert Hadley's direction in 1909, Vieth was among them too.

As a young man, Vieth worked for ten years under B.H. Pohl as a brickmaker and then for six years as a cooper for the Dulle Milling Company. Then, Vieth became bartender for William Wagner at the Monroe House. Using this knowledge, he and Christ Miller opened a liquor store on Madison Street and then purchased the City Hotel together. The newspaper described the duo as "young men of enterprise and pluck."

Miller continued to operate the City Hotel in 1896, when Vieth took over the Hotel Madison. That same year, Vieth was elected president of the newly organized Liquor Dealers Association, which promoted alcohol consumption in moderation and established a fund to relieve families of the sick and disabled.

New Hotel Madison

The New Hotel Madison was introduced to the community with a formal reception in early December 1900. A dance began at 9:30 p.m. in the Imperial Club Hall, which had been remodeled with new paint and paper, and the Jefferson City Orchestra played.

Keen to modernize the Hotel Madison, Vieth enlarged the lobby, creating a grand entrance and placing baths on every floor. The billiard hall wallpaper was replaced with hand-painted frescos.

Local architect Frank Miller designed a thirty-two-by-sixty-four-foot addition facing Main Street with galvanized iron bay windows the full height of the building.

The upper stories added twenty-four handsome bedrooms with brass bed stands and dedicated bathrooms. Most importantly, this project installed electricity throughout, setting up for the city's first elevator.

The main dining room on the second floor was thirty-one by sixty-three feet, plus a fourteen-by-thirty-foot private dining room. These were lighted on the north by three overhanging bay windows and featured panel work and frescoes. In the parlor was a mahogany Starr Grand piano with a "sweet tone and excellent finish."

The Hotel Madison received a full, modernized renovation in 1900. *Missouri State Archives.*

Vieth was elected president of the Missouri and Kansas Hotelmen's Association at its 1902 meeting in Kansas City. In 1909, he was named vice-president of the Northwestern Hotelmen's Association, without even attending the meeting held in the state of California. The newspaper asserted that Vieth was the "best known hotel man in the state" at the time.

More Improvements

By the spring of 1902, the Hotel Madison was five stories high on a 105-by-125-foot footprint, holding seventy-five rooms and seating for one hundred in the dining room. More improvements followed, with the removal of a street-access stairway to the second floor and installation of an interior grand stairway leading to spacious parlors and the reception hall.

The original stone steps leading to the first floor from street level were removed, and new, interior steps were installed. While excavating, workers found "rough hewn timbers" that were charred black, believed to be remnants from the previous Schmidt House foundation.

A portrait of namesake James Madison was part of the 1908 redecoration of the Hotel Madison dining rooms. *Missouri State Archives.*

The 1904 improvements featured a forty-foot-long balcony over the Madison Street sidewalk held up by iron columns and white marble, as well as walls of green and gold in the lobby.

The city's first elevator was installed at the Hotel Madison in early 1905. A special election in the fall of 1904 approved day service for electric lights in the city. That allowed Vieth to contract for the elevator. The downside was that the other fourteen thousand residents lost their electricity each time the elevator operated.

Another four-story addition west, including 23 new rooms, each with bath and modern conveniences, came in 1906. At this point, the Hotel Madison covered a quarter of a block and had 110 rooms.

The main dining room was redecorated in 1908, featuring a cartouche of fruit on the ceiling and Nile green and ivory panels. The walls were burnt orange and ecru. An oil portrait of the hotel's namesake, President James Madison, hung on the wall, and the polished floors were accented with Royal Wilton carpet between tables.

A ladies' parlor was added to the second floor, complete with satin upholstery and a baby grand piano. It featured floral design in shades of green and ivory with lace and silk draperies, designed by Wright-Gilmore Decorating Company of St. Louis, which also designed the Planters and Washington Hotels there.

In the basement were three barbers' chairs and four billiard tables. Vieth also added a new café and grill room with seating for forty-eight, using the European style of à la carte orders. The lobby of mahogany and marble was decorated with bric-a-brac and steins.

Vieth was always looking for the next modern marvel. Each room had long-distance telephone by 1906; in 1908, he had one of the first electric cash registers, and in 1909, a refrigerator was installed.

J.G. Bock

Vieth retired in January 1910, selling the hotel, furnishings, and the next-door airdome for $145,000 (about $4.8 million in 2025 dollars) to James Houchin, who also owned the Monroe House at the time. The airdome was a short-lived outdoor theater, popular across the Midwest in the early twentieth century.

Houchin then leased the operation to J.G. Bock, described as genial and affable, who had operated hotels in Minneapolis, Minnesota; St. Paul, Minnesota; Guthrie, Oklahoma; and Kansas City.

In 1910, the Jefferson City Taxicab Company opened an office at the news stand inside the Hotel Madison. The Underwood Typewriter Company hired stenographer Ethel Campbell to take public typing work at an office there.

When he made his bid for governor in 1912, Houchin set up his political headquarters at the hotel.

Jesse Palm

Jesse E. Palm of Wichita, Kansas, made a five-year lease with Houchin in 1913. Palm immediately hired Frank Miller to add another story to the hotel. This remodel introduced the Rathskellar in the fall of 1913, as well as two dining rooms and a tea room.

The cabaret-style Rathskellar in the basement had red, green, and gold designs. The floors were imported tile and the walls enameled green brick. Its walls featured bronze figures and oil paintings, and a large brick fireplace provided warmth. Private dining rooms adjoined it. The American dining room was converted into an "Oriental" tea room with marble floors and Circassian wainscoting. Live union musicians performed nightly. "It has witnessed many a gay scene in the past four years," the newspaper said when the Rathskellar closed, due to lack of patronage.

In 1917, Palm bought the two-hundred-room Lindell Hotel in Lincoln, Nebraska. While in Nebraska, Palm invented and patented the self-filling pencil, which he manufactured in 1926.

The W.R. Baker & Company, which also operated the O'Connor Hotel in Joplin, briefly held the lease. Then James A. Snyder took over for 1918–19. Snyder immediately painted the "drab" exterior red and installed an attractive electric Wurlitzer, which could make the sounds of seven instruments, in the restaurant.

W.B. "Billy" Smith

The next in the line of managers was Billy Smith, who came from Hot Springs, Arkansas. Smith was always accompanied by his bulldog, Boudie. The intelligent dog was known to carry newspapers to the traveling men who frequented the hotel.

With the Volstead Act and Prohibition on the horizon, the bar and café were converted into a coffee room, which catered to afternoon teas and evening parties. The old mahogany bar, where politicians had tipped their liquors while debating the issues, now served soft drinks and lunch. The dining room became the Peacock Room, where dances were held nightly.

The space once occupied by the Rathskellar was given to the Roscoe Enloe American Legion Post No. 5 as a meeting and club room in the fall of 1919. Just over a year later, the Legion moved into the third floor of the county courthouse.

Plans to develop the lot just west of the hotel, previously the site of the airdome, were revived in the summer of 1919, as Houchin directed Frank Miller to design a garage building with a roof garden. The next year, plans were made for this site to house a six-story apartment building. However, neither of these plans ever materialized.

In 1920, the former Central Hotel manager Bob Reaves and Foster McHenry took over management briefly.

Charles Kaiser

The Kaiser family returned to the Hotel Madison in 1922. Charles Kaiser along with his three siblings—John, Anne and Sophia Edwards—took over the lease. All of the children had grown up there.

Born in the City Hotel, Charles Kaiser knew the Hotel Madison as home from age two, and his first job at age fifteen was as day clerk. He worked for thirteen years in the hotel business before serving as chief clerk in the Missouri Pacific Railroad yards for five years. Until 1913, he was a traveling freight agent in Arkansas, and then he returned to Jefferson City, where he was appointed as State Board of Health statistician by Governors Frederick Gardner and Elliot Major.

When Houchin's property was seized after his Star Clothing Manufacturing Company failed, that included the Hotel Madison. An auction was held in June 1922, and Howard Cook bought the property and its debts for $46,000 (about $860,000 in 2025 dollars) on behalf of Myrene Houchin. Miss Houchin grew up in Jefferson City's affluent social world, with her father's wealth from prison factories and other investments. She continued to live at her family home at 611 Capitol Avenue with her husband, Jack Hobbs, a real estate investor. She was known for her horsemanship and involvement in the Cole County Historical Society.

Late in 1922, the ancient hitching post, which likely stood out front of the Hotel Madison for fifty years, was removed and the moment was mourned by local liveryman Clem Ware.

Charles Kaiser in 1927 made $50,000 (about $900,000 in 2025 dollars) in improvements, including converting restaurant space into guest rooms.

Rose and Levy

When the Kaisers' lease expired in 1929, Jack Hobbs leased the Hotel Madison to Louis Rose and Leo Levy, who had been operating hotels in the Midwest for years. At the time, the company also operated the Royal in Excelsior Springs and the Sexton in Kansas City. Charles Kaiser remained as manager, but he suffered a heart attack in the hotel lobby in 1932.

The Rose Hotel System invested $100,000 (about $1.8 million in 2025 dollars) into the renovations of the site, with ninety-two rooms and forty-eight baths. The exterior was finished in yellow, Spanish-style stucco, with green woodwork and an electric sign that advertised "Hotel Madison." It retained the arched windows, veranda, portico, and popular Capitol Avenue porches.

A new elevator and telephones in every room were included. The lobby and first floor were redesigned, creating the Madison McKenzie Coffee Shop. This was the third location for the Warrensburg brothers, who hired a former chef of the Tiger Hotel in Columbia.

Rose Hotel System made extensive renovations, including a Spanish-style stucco exterior finish, to the Hotel Madison in 1929. *Missouri State Archives.*

In the basement, a dry cleaning shop and Turkish baths and gymnasium were installed, as well as a photographer's studio and shoe company display rooms. The gymnasium was soon replaced with Sam Eveler's barber and beauty shop.

This corner had faced several fires in its one hundred years. The first to be fatal was in February 1931, when J.M. Schiltz of Wichita, Kansas, fell asleep with a lit cigarette in his fourth-floor room. Two others were injured in their escape, and a fireman was significantly injured during the response. One state representative was saved when a neighbor in the Missouri Power and Light building saw him signaling for help and provided a ladder. With the help of the prison fire department, the fire was suppressed before flames reached the attic of aged white pine.

With the repeal of Prohibition in December 1933, dancing and drinking in the former Rathskellar were revived. Remodeled and enlarged, the New Rathskellar had dining for ninety, plus three private dining rooms, a dance floor for forty couples, and a seven-piece orchestra for nightly floor shows.

In 1934, the "refrigerated Rathskellar" was one of the first places in the city with air conditioning. The Carrier Weathermaker maintained the temperature at seventy-eight degrees.

The McKenzie coffee bar was replaced by the Wonder Bar in 1935. The horseshoe-style bar had seating for 17 and built-in lounge booths for 110 in chrome and turquoise.

Leo Levy was the manager of the Rathskellar and Wonder Bar. He was in courts of various levels multiple times in 1934–36. The first was when the city demanded separate liquor licenses for the Rathskellar and the Wonder Bar, despite sharing the same address. Other violations included the sale of liquor on Sunday or sold after hours. One time, the bartender was caught rebottling a mixed drink. But all charges were dismissed or forgiven.

End of an Era

The first plan for razing the Hotel Madison came in the winter of 1937. By this time, Rose and Levy were managing thirty hotels and apartment houses, including the local Central Hotel. Rose and Levy had plans to build a new, modern 175-room hotel on the same corner with the same name.

Ironically, the same day Rose and Levy announced their plans, the newspaper also revealed that an out-of-town firm was planning an eleven-story, two-hundred-room Hotel Governor on the bluff at the southeast corner of State and Madison Streets, once the location of the city's first hotel, the Rising Sun.

Fate intervened to combine these projects when on May 4, 1939, the Hotel Madison was gutted in less than two hours by fire. The cause was dried cedar decorations and bunting left near the elevator shaft. Three men were significantly burned, and one died later.

Firefighters kept the fire from spreading to neighboring buildings, while trapped residents improvised exits. One man dropped a mattress out the window for his wife and self to jump onto, and another lady tied a bedsheet rope to reach a third-story fire escape from the fourth floor.

Mrs. Anna Baxter may have lost the most, as she had made the Hotel Madison her home for twenty years and had many heirlooms in her room. Firefighters did recover a $1,400 dinner ring in the debris directly below where her room would have been.

The Art Deco–styled Hotel Governor opened on this corner in 1942. It closed in the late 1980s, sitting vacant for a decade. The eight-story, twentieth-century hotel was renovated into today's ten-story Governor Office Building in 2000.

BIBLIOGRAPHY

Newspapers

California (MO) Democrat.
Central Missourian.
Concordia (KS) Press.
Current Local (Van Buren, MO).
Daily Capital News.
Daily Eclipse.
Daily Jefferson Inquirer.
Daily Missouri Republican.
Daily State Journal.
Examiner.
Galveston Daily News.
Glasgow Weekly Times.
Jefferson City (MO) Courier.
Jefferson City (MO) Daily Press.
Jefferson City (MO) Inquirer.
Jefferson City (MO) Peoples Tribune.
Jefferson City (MO) Post-Tribune.
Jefferson City (MO) Tribune.
Jeffersonian Republican (Jefferson City, MO).
Kansas City (MO) Times.
Kansas City (MO) World.
Macon (MO) Chronicle-Herald.

Missouri State Times.
Mosby's Missouri Message.
News and Tribune (Jefferson City, MO).
Niles National Register.
Republican Review.
Sedalia (MO) Democrat.
Sedalia (MO) Weekly Bazoo.
State Journal.
State Republican.
State Sentinel.
St. Louis (MO) Globe-Democrat.
St. Louis (MO) Republican.
St. Louis (MO) Star and Times.
Street Joseph (MO) Gazette.
Street Joseph (MO) Gazette-Herald.
Sturgeon Missouri Leader.
Sunday News Tribune.
Tipton Times.
Weekly Caucasian.
Weekly Jefferson Inquirer.
Weekly Springfield Advertiser.

Select Articles

Bolton, Theo J. *A Few of the Old-Time Druggists and "Apotheke" of Missouri.* Self-published, 1900.

Brooks, Michelle. "The Essence of the Munichburg Community." *Jefferson City (MO) News Tribune.* City Landmark series, July 17, 2016.

Brooks, Michelle. "From Hotel to Office Building, Its Name Is Constant: Governor." *Jefferson City (MO) News Tribune.* City Landmark series, October 21, 2012.

Brooks, Michelle. "Old Munichburg Renovation Earns Landmark Designation." *Jefferson City (MO) News Tribune.* City Landmark series, July 18, 2010.

Gensky, Henry. "Early Hotels of Jefferson City Were Renowned for Hospitality, Accommodations." *Jefferson City (MO) News Tribune*, April 9, 2022.

Goldammer, Deborah "Melody Farm, the Houchin Family 'Summer Home.'" *Jefferson City (MO) News Tribune.* Capital City History series, March 9, 2024.

Gunn, Calvin, Jr. "Jefferson City 65 Years Ago, Calvin Gunn Writes of Boyhood Days Here." *State Tribune*, May 14, 1902.

Keller, Rudi. "150 Years Ago: Emancipation Supporters Fail in Effort to Call New State Convention." *Columbia (MO) Tribune*, March 21, 2013.

Musick, Janet. "Jefferson City: An Architectural Biography." *Preservation Issues* (September 1995).

Priddy, Bob. "Inaugural Balls." January 9, 2017. https://bobpriddy.net/2017/01.

Rust, Mrs. Marshall. "Pioneer Homes and Early Mansions." *Sunday News and Tribune* (Jefferson City, MO), December 10, 1933.

Winn, Kenneth. "Missouri Taverns in Pioneer Days." *Current Local* (Van Buren, MO), May 27, 1943.

Winn, Kenneth. "One of Missouri's Richest Men Became City's First Mayor." *Yesterday and Today*, August 2011. Historic City of Jefferson.

Primary Sources

Beasley's Jefferson City Directory. 1877–78.

Bruns, Jette. *Hold Dear, as Always*. Edited by Adolph Schroeder. 2011.

A Business Directory of the Missouri Pacific, etc., St. Louis to Denver, for 1870.

Campbells Gazette. 1875.

City of Jefferson proclamation. February 26, 1842.

Cole County Circuit Court records.

Cole County Probate Court records.

Cole County Recorder of Deeds records.

Hoye's Jefferson City and Cole County Directory. 1904.

Hustings Court Deed Books. Lynchburg, Virginia.

Keemle, C. *Gazetteer of the State of Missouri*. 1837.

Logan's Railway Business Directory. 1873.

Missouri House Journals.

Missouri Permanent Seat of Government Commissioner's Report.

Missouri Provost Marshal Papers.

Missouri Senate Journals.

Missouri Session Laws.

Missouri State Archives, Permanent Seat of Government Collection.

Missouri State Archives Soldiers Database.

Missouri State Gazetteer and Business Directory for 1876–1877. St. Louis Mercantile Library.

Missouri State Gazetteer and Business Directory for 1881–1882. St. Louis Mercantile Library.

Missouri State Gazetteer and Business Directory for 1893–1894. St. Louis Mercantile Library.

Missouri State Gazetteer and Business Directory. 1860.

Montague's Missouri and Illinois Business Directory. 1854.

Parker, Nathan. *Missouri as It Is in 1867: An Illustrated Historical Gazetteer of Missouri*. 1867.
Phelps & Ensign's Traveller's Guide through the United States. New York, 1839.
Sanborn Fire Insurance Company Maps. Sanborn-Perris Map Company. Library of Congress.
Schroeder, Walter. *Munichburg Memories*. munichburgmemories.blogspot.com.
Tax Assessment Lists for Collection Districts in the State of Missouri, 1862–1865.
U.S. Census.
U.S. Passport Application.

Secondary Sources

Ancestry. "Colgan biography." ancestry.com.
Badzo, Bill. Flickr. 2012. www.flickr.com.
Basye, Otto. *The Basye Family in the United States*. Mid-State Printing Company, 1950.
The Basye House—Historical Sites Survey. Jefferson City Historic Houses vertical file. State Historical Society of Missouri.
Blevins, Robin. *Cole County Sheriff's Office and Jail History*. Self-published, 2018.
Brooks, Michelle, and Nancy Arnold Thompson. *Buried Jefferson City History*. Kindle Direct Publishing, 2022.
Brooks, Michelle. *Hidden History of Jefferson City*. The History Press, 2021.
Brooks, Michelle. *Murder & Mayhem Jefferson City*. The History Press, 2023.
Brooks, Michelle. *These Honored Dead: Jefferson City National Cemetery*. Kindle Direct Publishing, 2024.
Carnahan, Jean. *If Walls Could Talk*. Self-published, 1998. Financed for by the Missouri Mansion Preservation Inc.
Central Bank. "Central Bancompany History." www.centralbank.net.
City of Jefferson Landmark Awards. www.jeffersoncitymo.gov/live_play/history_heritage/landmark_awards.php.
ECCO Lounge. "Our History." www.eccolounge.net.
Ford, James. *History of Jefferson City*. New Day Press, 1938.
The History of Cole County, Missouri. Goodspeed Publishing Company, 1889.
Holmes, Patricia. "Lohman's Landing Building." National Register of Historic Places, 1969.
Isa, Mari. "The Great Oyster Craze: Why 19th Century Americans Loved Oysters." Michigan State University Campus Archaeology Program, 2017.
James, David. *Historic Hotels of Missouri: Hotels, Inns and Taverns of 19th Century Missouri*. Mira Digital Publishing, 2009.

Jefferson City Historic Southside Architectural Survey. Missouri State Parks, 1995.

Johnston, J.W. *Illustrated Sketchbook of Jefferson City and Cole County*. Tribune Printing Company, 1900.

Keller, Rudi. "Life During Wartime." Vol. 1. *Columbia Daily Tribune*, 2012.

Lansdown, Albert Young. *The Descendents of William Henry Lansdown*. New York, 1979.

Missouri Historical Review.

Missouri State Manual.

Missouri State Parks. "Jefferson Landing State Historic Site." www.mostateparks.com.

National Register of Historic Places. "Missouri State Capitol Historic District." 1974.

Patterson, Tiffany. Correspondence with author, 2024–25.

Priddy, Bob. *Across Our Wide Missouri*. Vols. 1–3. 1982.

Schroeder, Walter. *Breweries and Saloons in Jefferson City, Missouri*. Old Munichburg Association, 2011.

Stake, Louis. *Bohemian Brigade: Civil War Newsmen in Action*. Alfred Knopf Inc., 1954.

State Capital Cultural Resources Report. Missouri State Parks, 1990.

Swanberg, W.A. *Pulitzer*. Charles Scribner's Sons, 1967.

U.S. Biographical Dictionary and Portrait Gallery of Eminent and Self-Made Men. American Biographical Publishing Company, 1883.

UVA Unionists. "William Adams Curry." https://community.village.virginia.edu/unionist/node/738.

Young, Dr. Robert. *Pioneers of High, Water and Main: Reflections of Jefferson City*. Twelfth State, 1997

Repositories

Cole County Historical Society.

Kansas City Public Library.

Library of Congress.

Missouri State Archives.

Missouri State Library.

Missouri State Museum.

National Archives and Records Administration.

State Historical Society of Missouri.

INDEX

I've elected to list local married women by their more recognizable maiden name first, with their married names appearing in parentheses at the end.

C

D

E

F

G

H

I

J

K

L

M

S

T

U

V

W

Y

Z

ABOUT THE AUTHOR

Michelle Brooks is the author of seven other books: *Hidden History of Jefferson City*, *Lost Jefferson City*, *Murder & Mayhem Jefferson City*, and *Jefferson City Civil Pilots: From Lincoln University to Tuskegee Airmen* with The History Press; and *Interesting Women of the Capital City*, *Buried Jefferson City History*, and *These Honored Dead: Jefferson City National Cemetery*, published through Kindle Direct Publishing.

Her background includes a bachelor's degree from Lincoln University of Missouri with an emphasis in anthropology and history and nearly twenty-five years writing for Missouri newspapers. She is a research analyst at the Missouri State Archives.

Michelle is fascinated by the lesser-known stories in Jefferson City's local history and strives to make them accessible to future readers and history buffs. Future projects include an in-depth look at the individual soldiers of the Sixty-Second U.S. Colored Troops, who founded Lincoln University of Missouri and a retelling of the life of her grandfather Harry "HAP" Peebles, who was among the earliest country music promoters in the Midwest.

Also by Michelle Brooks

Buried Jefferson City History

Hidden History of Jefferson City

Interesting Women of the Capital City

Jefferson City Civil Pilots: From Lincoln University to Tuskegee Airmen

Lost Jefferson City

Murder & Mayhem Jefferson City

These Honored Dead: Jefferson City National Cemetery